TRUE CRIMES

DEADLY INTENT

igloo

igloo

This edition published in 2010
by Igloo Books Ltd
Cottage Farm
Sywell
NN6 0BJ

www.igloo-books.com

A copy of the British Library Cataloguing-in-Publication
Data is available from the British Library.

10 9 8 7 6 5 4 3 2 1

ISBN 978-0-85734-395-6

Printed and Manufactured in China

Contents

Ted Bundy

The total number will never be known, but at least 30 and as many as 100 unfortunate women and girls were victims of Ted Bundy during his four-year killing spree. That such a savage slayer seemed on the surface to be a handsome, dapper and charming man makes his case all the more compelling. So when did this all-American boy turn into a depraved monster?

Charmer With Movie Star Looks Was Merciless Manic

The answer may be earlier than anyone thought. When he was three years of age, Ted's 15-year-old aunt awoke one night to find that Ted had lifted the bedclothes and had placing butcher's knives around her body. 'He just stood there and grinned,' she recalled. 'I shooed him out of the room and took the knives back to the kitchen. I remember thinking at the time that it was a very strange thing for a little kid to do.'

Young Theodore Robert was living with his grandparents at the time. Born on November 24, 1946, to an unmarried teenage mother in Philadelphia, he took on the name Bundy when she moved to Washington State in 1950 and wed hospital cook Johnnie Bundy. The bridegroom adopted Ted as his own son and he grew up with them in their Tacoma home in apparent domestic harmony.

Young Bundy became the all-American boy, joining the Boy Scouts, having a paper round and doing backyard clearance and mowing jobs for pocket money. His school grades were good and he was a high school athlete, then a student at the University of Washington. He became a campaign worker both for the Republican Party and for the Crime Commission in Washington State, where former colleagues believed he could have ended up a leading lawyer, a top politician, perhaps even a Senator.

But further clues to his character had arisen. His student reports spoke of a volatile temper. And although his undeniable charm and movie star looks won him no shortage of dates, some girlfriends recalled him as a sadistic lover who acted out weird bondage fantasies. Nevertheless, in 1971 he applied for voluntary work at a Seattle rape crisis center and, after being screened for

LEFT: The many faces of prolific American serial killer, Ted Bundy— all of them evil.

ABOVE: Bundy at one of many court appearances. During one, in Aspen, Colorado, he leapt from a window and escaped.

vanished from her Seattle apartment on the morning of January 31, 1974, leaving only a bloodstain on her pillow as a clue to her kidnapping and murder. Over the next three months, three more students, all teenagers, and two other women had been abducted and killed.

By mid-1974, Bundy, then aged 28, had become sufficiently emboldened to operate by daylight and even to give his real name, introducing himself with: 'Hi, I'm Ted.' In July, the killer, with his arm in a sling, wandered among a crowd of 40,000 who were swimming and sunbathing at Lake Sammamish State Park, near Seattle, approaching young girls and asking if they would help with his sailboat. One who declined nevertheless watched as the man—'really friendly, very polite, very sincere, with a nice smile'—lured another girl to his distinctive VW Beetle car. He killed two women that day, their naked bodies found in woodland months later, along with those of three other women, one a known missing person and two unidentifiable.

'maturity and balance', he was accepted as a counsellor.

It was this innocent image that Bundy played up to when he finally faced his accusers in a series of court appearances starting in 1975, during which the smiling, smooth-talker tried to charm jurors into believing he had no need to kidnap and kill. As he boasted: 'Why should I want to attack women? I had all the female companionship I wanted. I must have slept with dozens and all of them went to bed with me willingly.'

Even today, the mystery remains as to the total number of murders Bundy committed: the nine murders with which he was officially attributed, the 20 to 30 to which he had confessed or the 100-plus with which some investigators credit him, the general estimate being 35.

The manner of these deaths was not gentle. Typically, Bundy would bludgeon his victims, then strangle them to death. He also engaged in rape and necrophilia. His first known victim was law student Lynda Ann Healy, 21, who

ABOVE: Bundy stalled his execution for 10 years, but eventually went to the electric chair in February 1989.

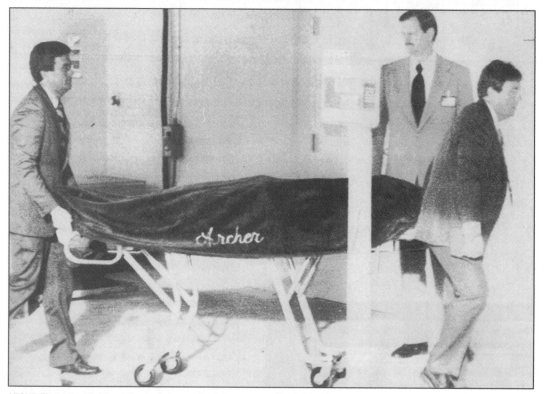

ABOVE: The body of Ted Bundy is wheeled away after he was executed in the electric chair at Starke Prison, Florida, on January 24, 1989.

But the trail in Washington went cold when Bundy moved state, enrolling at the University of Utah law school in Salt Lake City. There, in October and November, four girls aged between 16 and 18 were abducted, battered, raped, and strangled. The slaughter spread from Utah to Colorado, where between January and April 1975 at least five women went missing.

Police finally nabbed Bundy in Salt Lake City one night in August 1975—but initially only for a traffic violation. He was driving his VW with no lights when stopped and found to be in possession of a pair of handcuffs, a crowbar, a ski mask, and a nylon stocking. Charged with possessing tools for burglary, he was put in an identity line-up and was picked out by one of his would-be victims, 18-year-old Carol Da Ronch. She'd had a lucky escape when Bundy, posing as a police officer, had handcuffed her and dragged her into his VW, from which she rolled out as it slowed at a bend.

Bundy was charged with kidnapping but after months of legal argument—during much of which, incredibly, he was allowed out on bail—he was found guilty and sentenced to between one and 15 years. He was then moved to Colorado to stand trial for the murder of a 23-year-old student, abducted from a ski resort in January.

During a break in the court hearing at Aspen, Bundy leaped from a window and was free for eight days before recapture. He escaped a second time by cutting through a ceiling panel of his cell and stealing a police car. Driving first to Chicago, then traveling south to

Florida, Bundy rented a room near the University of Florida, Tallahassee, and again went on the rampage. On January 15, 1978, he crept into a dormitory at the university and viciously battered four students, strangling two of them to death before taking bites out of the buttocks of one of them.

Bundy's last victim was his youngest. On February 8, in Lake City, Florida, 12-year-old Kimberly Leach was strangled and sexually violated. A week later, when a Pensacola policeman stopped him for driving a stolen car, the killer tried to escape but was clubbed unconscious. He was brought to trial in Miami and convicted of the Tallahassee student murders and subsequently, in 1980, of the murder of young Kimberly Leach.

Bundy stalled his execution for almost 10 years with a string of appeals but finally confessed to 30 murders, including attacks in California, Michigan, Pennsylvania, Idaho, and Vermont. He went to the electric chair in Florida's Starke Prison in January 1989.

John Bunting and accomplices

On May 21, 1999, Adelaide police reopened a missing persons investigation that led them to a disused bank vault in rural Snowtown, South Australia. What they found there was a chamber of horrors that would stun the nation. Six acid-filled plastic barrels contained the grisly, mummified remains of eight dismembered bodies. Three days later, two further bodies were found buried in a backyard in a suburb north of Adelaide. A day later, four men were arrested, and the search for justice began.

Dismembered Bodies In Chamber Of Horrors

Former abattoir worker John Justin Bunting, born in Queensland in 1966, was the ringleader of a dysfunctional group of victims of child sex abuse and incest who shared an overriding hatred for homosexuals and pedophiles. Bunting, a psychopathic killer, and himself a victim of childhood sexual abuse, enlisted the help of friends (Robert Wagner and Mark Haydon, Bunting's second wife Elizabeth Harvey and stepson James Vlassakis) to partake in various acts of abduction, torture, and disposal of bodies.

Usually based on flimsy evidence or rumor, victims were murdered if suspected of being pedophiles. Others were killed because they were obese, illiterate, mentally disabled, gay or drug addicted. Most of the victims were friends, acquaintances or family members of at least one of the group.

Although not the motive for the killings, the murderers took on the identity of their victims to claim their welfare benefits, forging their signatures to pocket $95,000 and in some cases 'inheriting' their cars.

Bunting's killing spree began in August 1992. Clinton Trezise, 22, was struck about the head with a hammer several times in Bunting's living room after being invited round for a social visit.

For the next seven years, Bunting and his accomplices took the lives of various men and women—using torture methods such as electric clamps, pliers, cigarettes, and lit sparklers inserted in the penis in order to 'cure' their victims of their crimes. The victims were forced to call their torturers 'God', 'Master', 'Chief Inspector', and 'Lord Sir'.

Among the death toll was Suzanne Allen, 47, a friend of Bunting; Elizabeth Haydon, 37, wife of one of Bunting's co-conspirators; and Thomas Trevilyan, 18, who had helped murder one victim but was later killed after discussing the crime with others. In September 1998, Bunting's stepson, James Vlassakis, was persuaded to participate in the murder of his own half-brother

Troy Youde, just 21, who was killed in his house after being dragged from his bed while asleep.

David Johnson, 24, was the last to be murdered, in May 1999. He was lured to the disused bank with the promise of a low-price computer. There he was handcuffed and made to give his bank details. Two of the killers left to confirm the details were correct and Bunting strangled Johnson before they returned.

In the final stages of a complex, year-long missing persons investigation, police entered the former Snowtown branch of the State Bank of South Australia after a tip-off from neighbors. The discovery there of the eight dismembered bodies horrified hardened cops. Days later, two more bodies were uncovered at Bunting's former house and were linked to the same killers. Bunting, Haydon, Wagner, and Vlassakis were arrested and charged with murder.

After 11 months of shocking evidence in South Australia's longest and most complex criminal trial, the jury returned a guilty verdict against John Bunting and Robert Wagner. The jury found Bunting killed 11 people while his accomplice, Wagner, a bisexual muscleman, murdered seven. They were each sentenced to life imprisonment on each count, to be served cumulatively. The presiding judge, Justice Brian Martin, said the men were 'in the business of killing for pleasure' and were 'incapable of true rehabilitation'.

In a separate trial in the Adelaide Supreme Court, 22-year-old James Vlassakis, pleaded guilty to four counts of murder and was handed a life sentence with a 26-year non-parole period.

The proceedings against Mark Haydon continued into September 2005, when murder charges against him were dropped in return for guilty pleas to charges of assisting in the killings, including that of his wife, Elizabeth.

The convictions proved what South Australians first gathered four years previously: that a group of sadistic killers had operated unchecked in their midst for most of the previous decade. Finally, their reign of terror had been brought to an end.

Angelo Buono and Kenneth Bianchi

Kenneth Bianchi, born to an alcoholic prostitute who gave him up at birth, was deeply troubled from a young age. His adoptive mother described him as 'a compulsive liar who had risen from the cradle dissembling'. After a brief marriage to his high school sweetheart, he drifted from New York State to California, where in 1977 he teamed up with his older cousin Angelo Buono Jr. — and together they became known as the Hillside Stranglers.

Raped, Tortured, And Slain By The 'Hillside Stranglers'

Buono was an ugly man, both physically and mentally. He was coarse, ignorant, and sadistic but, incredibly, was popular with women and gave himself the nickname 'Italian Stallion'. Also from Rochester, New York, he had moved to California with his divorced mother and, like Bianchi, he briefly married a young girlfriend before walking out on her and their baby.

Between brief spells in jail for theft, Buono again wed and fathered several further children in and out of wedlock before his wife divorced him after he handcuffed her, put a gun to her stomach and threatened to kill her.

Buono worked as a car upholsterer, carrying out his business from his home at Glendale, in the San Fernando Valley. It was there that younger cousin Bianchi joined him and the couple, then aged 42 and 26, regularly invited prostitutes to the house. It would be these who would become their first victims.

ABOVE: Kenneth Bianchi and his older cousin stripped, raped, and sometimes sodomized their victims.

they were certain to be discovered, often displayed in lascivious postures.

After the third murder, police knew that two men had been involved. The evidence was sperm samples taken from the teenager's body. As further corpses turned up, police also realized that the killers were experimenting with forms of torture. After being abused by both men, the girls would be strangled. But other methods of killing, such as lethal injection, electric shock, and carbon monoxide poisoning, were also tried by the killers.

During one week in November, Bianchi and Buono disposed of five bodies, the youngest being of

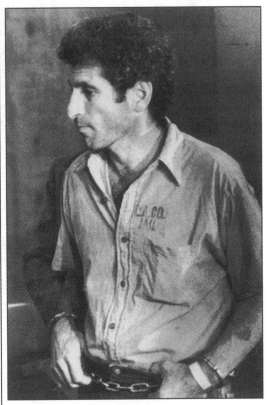

ABOVE: The self styled 'Italian Stallion', Angelo Buono committed his first murder in October 1977.

The body of a 21-year-old Hollywood girl was found on a hillside on Chevy Chase Drive on October 6, 1977. Twelve days later, the body of a 19-year-old was dumped near the Forest Lawn Cemetery. And on October 31, a girl aged just 15 was found dead on a hillside in Glendale.

A pattern had emerged. The girls had been stripped naked, violently raped, and sometimes sodomized. They were then carefully cleaned by the killers so as to leave no clues. Finally they were dumped by roadsides where

ABOVE: Bianchi takes the stand during his trial. His claim of insanity saved him from the death penalty.

schoolgirls aged 12 and 14. Two more teenagers and another woman were killed before the end of the year, and a 20-year-old died the following February.

The deadly duo lured their victims by cruising around Los Angeles in Buono's car pretending to be plain-clothes cops, stopping to flash fake badges at unsuspecting victims. Ordered into their 'unmarked police car', the girls were driven to Buono's home to be tortured and murdered. But in the spring of 1978, to the bafflement of Los Angeles police, the killings suddenly stopped.

The reason was that the killers had fallen out, and Bianchi had left California to live with his girlfriend and baby son in Bellingham, Washington State. There, Bianchi took a job as a security guard, and in January 1979 he lured two girl students into a house he was guarding and strangled them. But without the aid of his partner, he left many clues and police arrested him the next day. The nature of the crime and several documents in his possession linked him with the Hillside Strangler cases.

At his trial for the two Bellingham murders, Bianchi pleaded insanity, claiming that he suffered from 'multi personality disorder', and the evidence of six Washington State psychiatrists saved him from the death penalty. With a life sentence, he was moved to California to give evidence against Buono for the Los Angeles killings.

The inadmissibility of 'insane' Bianchi's testimony delayed the start of Buono's trial until November 1981 and, along with the lack of forensic evidence, caused it to last nearly two years. Buono denied all charges and blamed the murders on his cousin. On October 31, 1983, he was found guilty on two counts—but the jury's recommendation meant that he too evaded the death sentence in favor of life in prison, where he died of a heart condition in 2002.

At the close of his trial, it became clear that Judge Ronald George would have preferred Buono's death to have been administered more swiftly. He complained to the jury: 'Angelo Buono and Kenneth Bianchi subjected various of their murder victims to the administration of lethal gas, electrocution, strangulation by rope, and lethal hypodermic injection. Yet the two defendants are destined to spend their lives in prison, housed, fed, and clothed at taxpayer expense, better cared for than some of the destitute law-abiding members of our community.'

William Burke and William Hare

In the early 19th century, the frontiers of medicine were advancing at an inexorable rate. Yet there was one vital ingredient lacking in this exploration of the human body—and that was a supply of the bodies themselves. At that time, it was unheard of for anyone to donate their body for research, so a supply of corpses had to be provided for dissection and the fresher the better. William Burke and William Hare were the men to fulfill this service, and by their nefarious trade became Scotland's most celebrated and gruesome serial murderers.

Unholy Duo Who Went Into The 'Body Business'

The Irish-born pair came together when Burke, who had deserted his wife and young family, came to stay at Hare's cheap Edinburgh lodging house in 1827. They went into the 'body business' together soon afterward upon the death of a boarder known as Old Donald, who succumbed to a long illness, owing £4 in rent. To recoup his loss, landlord Hare hit upon the plan of selling the corpse to one of the city's doctors. They removed Old Donald's body from the coffin that lay in the backyard, wrapped it in sacking and presented themselves at the door of Number 10 Surgeons' Square, the Edinburgh establishment of the brilliant anatomist Dr Robert Knox. The price was struck at seven pounds and 10 shillings, and all sides left well satisfied with the night's work.

It was easy money but the pair realized they would have difficulty in continually restocking the merchandise they required for their new unholy trade. Churchyards were now well guarded at night because of previous raids by grave robbers, and many tombs even had iron bars around them. The only solution was to 'create' new corpses.

The first of a further 16 victims was an old man called Joe the Mumper, who fell ill of a high fever and was too weak to offer resistance as Burke and Hare laid a pillow over his face and held him down until he suffocated. His body fetched £10 at Surgeons' Square. The second victim was dispatched in what became the hallmark of Burke and Hare's murder technique. A boarder, whose name they did not even know, was confined to his bed with jaundice. While the man was asleep, Burke held his mouth and nose until there was no sign of breathing.

Third to die was an old woman tramp whom Hare met in a city bar, lured to the lodging house and suffocated. In the spring of 1828, the killers saw off two more boarders, both destitute women. Then came the murder of a prostitute, Mary Paterson. The sight of her naked body, barely six hours into death, aroused great excitement among the medical students, one of whom claimed to recognize her. Mary's shapely figure and good looks were even remarked upon in the popular newspapers. Dr Knox gladly reveled in the publicity and, rather than take the body straight onto the dissecting table, he had it preserved in whiskey for three months, allowing it to become almost a tourist attraction.

Burke and Hare became increasingly audacious. On one occasion, Burke encountered a drunken woman being escorted along the street by a policeman. He intervened, convinced the officer that he was a Good Samaritan and had the hapless wretch released into his care. Not surprisingly, she was delivered to Surgeons' Square that very night.

In June 1828, the partners committed their vilest crime. Burke was stopped in the street and asked for directions by a woman leading by the hand a young boy who was deaf and dumb. Burke led her to his home where he and Hare killed her before also disposing of her son. Burke took the boy over his knee and, as he later told police, 'broke his back' while the terrified youngster stared piteously into his face. The two victims were then stuffed into a barrel and sold for £16 the pair.

In the end, Burke and Hare were trapped by their over-confidence and carelessness. In October 1828, a female boarder turned up the corner of her straw mattress and was horrified to discover the body of a

ABOVE LEFT: Notorious Scottish murderer William Burke, as he appeared in court. Burke, with his accomplice William Hare, murdered nine people, selling the bodies to medical schools for dissection.

ABOVE RIGHT: William Hare was an accomplice of William Burke and Robert Knox. Burke was hanged for his crimes but Hare gave evidence and was released with Robert Knox.

ABOVE: An angry mob pursues Helen MacDougal, mistress of serial killer William Burke, through the streets of Edinburgh, circa 1829.

naked crone, her face horribly bloodstained. She went to the police and the killers were arrested. Hare, given an offer of immunity by turning King's Evidence, immediately denounced his former partner.

The trial of William Burke began on Christmas Eve 1828 and continued without pause until the last guilty verdict was returned on Christmas morning. The court's sentence was that he be hanged and his body be used for medical science. A crowd of thousands, among them the poet Walter Scott, watched him die on the gallows on January 28, 1829.

Burke's body was then removed to the medical rooms, where guests were admitted in batches of 50 to watch it being dissected. The following day, the general public was admitted, thousands of curious strangers filing past his remains. The body was then salted and put into barrels for use in future experiments.

Only Burke suffered the full weight of the law but the other players in the vile pantomime did not enjoy their freedom. The infamous Dr Knox continued to deny complicity in the crimes but found his medical career in ruins. He died in disgrace in December 1862. The wives of Burke and Hare, who assisted the pair in their vile trade, suffered public hatred wherever they went. And Hare himself, having turned against his accomplice to obtain his own freedom, moved away from Edinburgh and lived out a miserable existence in the slums of London, eventually dying a poverty-stricken blind beggar.

ABOVE: Crowds gather to watch the execution of William Burke at the Lawnmarket, Edinburgh, on January 28, 1829.

David Carpenter

The so-called 'Trailside Killings' in the San Francisco Bay Area began in August 1979 with the murder of 44-year-old Edda Kane, who had been hiking in Mount Tamalpais State Park. She was raped and then shot through the back of the head while kneeling.

Stuttering Psycho Known As The 'Trailside Killer'

Seven months later, 23-year-old Barbara Schwartz was stabbed while on her knees. Then came Anne Alderson, a 26-year-old jogger, found dead in the park with three bullets in her head. She, too, had been in the kneeling position at the time of her death.

ABOVE: Mount Tamalpais State Park, where David Carpenter carried out the 'Trailside Killings'.

wounds. Blake's description allowed police to release a composite picture of the killer.

The net was closing in on the 'Trailside Killer'—but not before he had claimed a final victim. In May, Heather Skaggs, 20, was found dead in Big Basin Redwood State Park. Bullets used to kill her matched those fired at Gene Blake and Ellen Hansen. But now there were further clues. Heather had worked in the same print store as a known sex offender, David Carpenter, she had last been seen near his home—and work colleagues said they believed Carpenter had tried to date her.

The trail clearly led to the man who should have been a suspect from the start. Carpenter was a psycho with a pronounced stutter who, in 1960 at the age of 30, had been arrested and sentenced to 14 years in prison for attacking a woman with a hammer and knife. Freed early, he re-offended in 1970 and spent seven years in jail for kidnapping. In between his two prison terms, he had been a principal suspect in California's mysterious 'Zodiac murders' (see page 219) but was ultimately cleared.

Indeed, one other murder victim may have preceded the uproar over the 'Trailside Killings'. Anna Menjivas, who had been a friend of Carpenter's, disappeared from her home in 1979 and was found dead in Mount Tamalpais Park, the area of the next three murders. Yet police failed to link her death to Carpenter until after his arrest.

On July 6, 1984, Carpenter was found guilty in Los Angeles of the murders of Heather Scaggs and Ellen Hansen. He was sentenced to death in the gas chamber of San Quentin. At a second trial in San Diego, Carpenter was convicted of five more murders and two rapes and again sentenced to death, but a string of appeals meant he languished indefinitely on Death Row.

The killer went into overdrive in late 1980. Hiker Shawna May, 25, was shot and placed in a shallow grave in Point Reyes Park. Nearby was the body of another missing person, Diane O'Connell, 22, also shot in the head. On the same day, November 29, two more bodies were found in Point Reyes: Cynthia Moreland, 18, and Richard Towers, 19, had been killed on the same October weekend as Alderson.

The discovery of four bodies in one day caused a howl of outrage in the media and spread fear across the Bay Area, where jogging, hiking, and other healthy outdoor activities were a way of life. However, police had few leads to follow. No one had seen the mysterious 'Trailside Killer' and survived.

Then, in March 1981, hitch-hikers Ellen Hansen and Gene Blake were threatened at gunpoint in a park near Santa Cruz. She was shot dead, but her boyfriend managed to crawl away, bleeding profusely from his

Andrei Chikatilo

Crazed cannibal Andrei Chikatilo was questioned several times during his 12 years of slaughter and released on every occasion. The mild-mannered former schoolteacher convinced detectives that he was a faithful husband, proud father, and studious academic.

'Rostov Ripper' Killed And Ate More Than 50

A university graduate, Chikatilo completed his military service and in 1963, at the age of 27, he met and married Fayina, a pit worker's daughter. They had a son and a daughter as Chikatilo continued his home studies, gaining a degree in literature and taking a job as a teacher. For reasons no one then guessed, he gave up the post in 1981 and started work as a supply clerk, a humble job but one that involved much travel.

This gave him greater scope for his perverted pleasures, for Chikatilo was already a killer. Although living in an apartment in Rostov-on-Don, Russia, he had also bought a dilapidated shack outside the town, to which he regularly brought back prostitutes for sex. In December 1978, he lured a nine-year-old girl there and, following a failed attempt at rape, brutally stabbed her to death.

It transpired from his wife's later evidence that Chikatilo could not have sex in any normal way. He needed to instil terror before he could perform adequately. He would rape his victims only after working himself into a frenzy as he stabbed and mutilated them.

He went on to kill at least 53 people around Rostov and as far afield as St Petersburg and Tashkent, Uzbekistan. He would hang around bus stops and railroad stations, stalking his victims, mainly targeting prostitutes, tramps or runaways, whom he lured with the promise of gifts or a meal.

Most of his victims were raped after death and then mutilated, with various organs cut out or bitten off. He would often consume their flesh. His oldest victim was a 44-year-old prostitute and his youngest a seven-year-old boy. There was also a mother and her 11-year-old daughter, who vanished after he took them on a picnic.

'I paid no attention to age or sex,' he later told police, adding: 'Eating my victims is the ultimate sacrifice they can make for me. They are literally giving themselves to me.'

Chikatilo avoided capture because of police

ABOVE: Andrei Chikatilo behind the bars of an iron cage during his trial in Rostov in 1992.

blunders. He was arrested after his very first murder when neighbors reported strange happenings at his shack. During the 12-year hunt for the so-called 'Rostov Ripper', he was questioned by police on at least eight further occasions, on one of them being kept in custody for 10 days. They even closed the case briefly when inquiries switched to another suspect—who, bizarrely, confessed to murder and was executed.

The killings did in fact cease for three months. That was because Chikatilo had been sent to prison, not for any violent crime but on an old charge of stealing linoleum. After his release, he slaughtered eight people in a single month.

Chikatilo was finally arrested outside a cafe in November 1990. He admitted murdering 11 boys and 42 girls but police believe there may have been more. He went on trial chained in an iron cage within the Rostov courtroom where, in October 1992, he was sentenced to death. He was executed with a bullet in the back of the neck on February 14, 1994.

ABOVE: Chikatilo relished cannibalism. He once said that eating his victims is 'the ultimate sacrifice they can make for me'.

John Reginald Christie

In the annals of British crime, few addresses are more enduringly spine-chilling than 10 Rillington Place, in London's Notting Hill district. Now trendily upgraded, the area was, in the postwar years, distinctly shabby and seedy. It is a description that could equally have applied to one of the occupants: the balding, bespectacled John Reginald Halliday Christie.

The Chilling Secret of 10 Rillington Place

Christie committed at least six and possibly eight murders in his rented ground-floor apartment there, hiding the corpses around the house as a gruesome legacy for the next tenant to find. One body was of a woman for whose death her husband was wrongly sent to the gallows.

Born in Halifax, Yorkshire, in 1898, Christie was a weakly youth who nevertheless enlisted in World War One and suffered eye and throat injuries in a mustard gas attack. He returned home with a small disability pension, married a local girl and went to work for the Post Office.

This was where his life of crime began, for he was caught stealing postal orders and was sent to jail, the first of several spells behind bars for what were, at first, petty offenses. When wife Ethel discovered he was also visiting prostitutes, Christie moved alone to London, where he served three further jail terms for theft and attacking a woman.

ABOVE: John Christie was first jailed for stealing postal orders, but his criminal activities soon escalated to murder by strangulation.

BELOW: Austrian refugee Ruth Fuerst, who was murdered by Christie in 1943 and buried in his backyard.

After a nine-year separation, he wrote to Ethel seeking a reconciliation, and in 1938 they moved into 10 Rillington Place. Extraordinarily, World War Two saw him back into uniform as a police special constable, no checks having been made for previous convictions. Under that guise of authority and respectability, he began murdering women.

In 1943, he picked up a 17-year-old Austrian refugee, took her back to Rillington Place while his wife was absent and strangled her with a rope. Under cover of darkness, he buried her body in the small communal backyard, where it lay undisturbed for a decade.

After losing his police post the following year, Christie worked at various clerking jobs, in one of which he chatted up a 31-year-old co-worker and invited her to his home. There, he raped and strangled her with a stocking and buried her alongside his first victim.

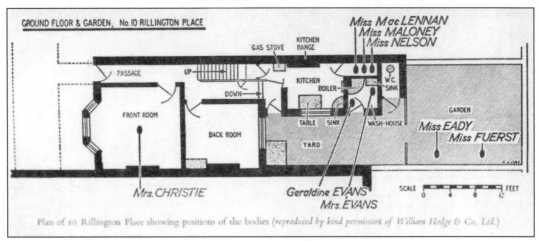

GROUND FLOOR & GARDEN, No. IO RILLINGTON PLACE

Miss MacLENNAN
Miss MALONEY
Miss NELSON

GAS STOVE

KITCHEN RANGE

PASSAGE

UP

DOWN

KITCHEN

BOILER

W.C.

SINK

GARDEN

Miss EADY
Miss FUERST

FRONT ROOM

BACK ROOM

TABLE   SINK

YARD

WASH-HOUSE

SCALE
0   4   8   12   FEET

Mrs. CHRISTIE

Geraldine EVANS
Mrs. EVANS

Plan of 10 Rillington Place showing positions of the bodies (*reproduced by kind permission of William Hodge & Co., Ltd.*)

ABOVE: A plan of Christie's apartment of evil, showing the locations in which his victims were buried.
BELOW: Christie's 'murder room', situated at the rear of his ground-floor apartment.

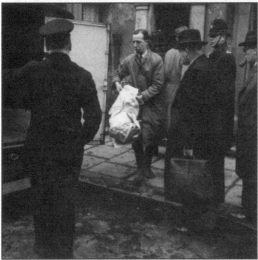

In 1948 truck driver Timothy Evans, his wife Beryl, and their baby Geraldine moved into the apartment above Christie's. A year later, Beryl and 14-month-old Geraldine were murdered. Inexplicably, Evans, who was of subnormal intelligence, went to the police to confess to killing his wife—but when they raided the house and also found his daughter's body, he changed his story, blaming his neighbor. Christie gave evidence against Evans, sealing his fate. He was hanged on March 9, 1950.

Christie's next victim was his wife. In 1952 he strangled Ethel in bed and buried her under the floorboards. That left him free to bring prostitutes to the apartment, three of whom he murdered and stuffed

LEFT: The bones of Christie's fifth victim are removed from 10 Rillington Place by police.

into cupboards. In March 1953, he moved out of Rillington Place and lived rough. Within days he was arrested after the apartment's next tenant discovered the grisly cause of the stench that permeated the house.

At London's Old Bailey, Christie's plea of insanity was rejected and on July 15, 1953, he was hanged for four

of the murders, including that of Ethel. But who killed Beryl Evans? Christie finally confessed to her murder but two subsequent tribunals failed to overturn the verdict against Timothy Evans. In 1966, however, the lingering doubts earned Evans a long-overdue posthumous royal pardon.

Douglas Clark and Carol Bundy

Douglas Clark, the 'Sunset Strip Slayer', had a particularly gruesome fetish. He killed prostitutes, one of whom he decapitated and had sex with her head. His girlfriend Carol Bundy indulged this perversion by applying make-up to the head. Clark kept this grisly memento in his freezer for a few days, taking it out from time to time for the purpose of oral sex.

Hideous Habits Of The 'Sunset Strip Slayer'

Clark, handsome son of a former admiral in the US Navy, was 31 when, in 1980, he met Bundy, a dumpy 37-year-old mother of two, who worked as a vocational nurse in Los Angeles. He moved into her apartment in Burbank and made her his willing sex slave. He brought women and girls, as young as 11, home for sex while she watched and photographed them.

Then, in June 1980, the bodies of stepsisters aged 15 and 16 were found beside a highway. They had been snatched by Clark from Huntington Beach and forced to perform sex acts before being shot in the head. Although Bundy may not have been involved in that crime, she was an active participant in those that followed.

She and Clark would regularly drive along Sunset Boulevard to pick up a prostitute. Once parked in a quiet street, Clark would force her to perform oral sex on him while Bundy watched. As he climaxed, Clark would shoot the girl in the head.

Their murderously kinky games resulted in the bodies of prostitutes aged 17, 20, and 24 turning up during their June killing spree. Each had been disposed of in the

same manner—except that in the case of the 20-year-old, her head was missing. It was found three days later in a box in the driveway of a house in Hollywood.

According to Bundy's later testimony, Clark had taken the head home with him so he could engage in oral sex with it at his leisure. She said that while her two children were out, Clark had produced the head from the freezer, ordered her to comb the hair and apply make-up to it. 'We had a lot of fun with her,' she told police. 'I was making her up like a Barbie.'

Clark's next victim was never identified. Her dismembered body turned up in Malibu in July. The final murder victim died the following month at the hands of Bundy herself. He was a former boyfriend, barman John Murray, who had foolishly confided to her that he suspected her new lover might be the 'Sunset Strip Slayer'. Bundy set up a meeting at which she shot and stabbed him, then decapitated him. His torso was discovered in his van but his head was never found.

Bundy may have been trying to prove to Clark her equal ability to kill but she could not carry it off. The overweight, mentally disturbed nurse broke down and confessed to a colleague. Police were tipped off and the killers were arrested. After initially blaming each other, Bundy confessed her involvement in the crimes, pleading guilty to the murder of Murray. Sentenced to

ABOVE: Sunset Strip in Los Angeles, the hunting ground of Douglas Clark and Carol Bundy during the summer of 1980.

life imprisonment, she became key witness against her boyfriend at his 1983 trial.

Clark was found guilty on six counts of murder and was sentenced to death. The Californian Supreme Court affirmed the sentence in 1992, leaving the 'Sunset Strip Slayer' lingering on Death Row— surviving his partner Bundy, who died in prison of heart failure in December 2003.

Adolfo Constanzo

Adolfo de Jesus Constanzo was a practitioner of voodoo for the power it gave him over others. He was also a devotee of the strange religion because it allowed him to satiate his bloodlust with regular human sacrifices.

Human Sacrifices Of The Voodoo Cult

Born in Miami of Cuban extraction in 1962, Constanzo studied the black magic arts of Palo Mayombe, a violent sect imported from the Congo. The cult believes the spirits of the dead exist in limbo and can be harnessed if the gods are regularly appeased with the fresh blood of human sacrifices. Constanzo would keep a cauldron constantly filled with blood and, most importantly, the skull of a human who had died a violent death.

At the age of 21, Constanzo moved to Mexico City where in 1983 he launched himself as a Palo Mayombe priest. Superstitious drugs family godfathers turned to him for magical protection at $50,000 a spell. As a consequence, his cauldron needed constant replenishment with fresh blood and skulls, and decapitated corpses were regularly fished out of rivers and lakes by police. On one occasion, the mutilated bodies of five members of the same household were discovered.

Constanzo's method of sacrifice was to have the victim beaten, then dragged to the sacred cauldron. It was essential to the success of the ceremony that there should be as much pain as possible and the victim should die screaming. So Constanzo would cut off the nose, ears, fingers, toes, and genitals of the hapless wretch

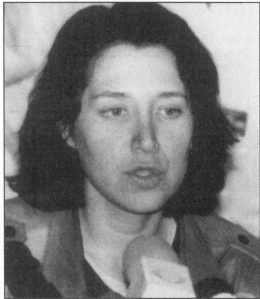

ABOVE: Sara Aldrete, a member of Constanzo's evil cult, was sentenced to 62 years without parole in 1994.

ABOVE: Adolfo Constanzo's obsession with the black magic arts of Palo Mayombe drove him to make many human sacrifices.

and partially flay him before sodomizing him. Only then would there be a merciful release through death.

Constanzo moved his voodoo circle to Matamoros, near the Texan border, where between May 1988 and March 1989 the gang ritually sacrificed at least 13 people. They were often rival drug dealers but also included strangers picked up at random.

Mark Kilroy was just such a victim. The 21-year-old medical student had crossed the border with friends to celebrate the end of their university term. When he became separated from them, he was bundled into the back of a truck and driven to Constanzo's remote Santa Elena ranch, where he was butchered and his brains tipped into the cauldron.

Kilroy's worried parents agitated for a properly conducted police investigation, and success was swift. Mexican police set up a road block near Matamoros, and one of Constanzo's gang drove straight through it—having been told by his leader that he was invisible! The cops simply followed him to the ranch, where they unearthed human remains including those of Mark Kilroy.

Constanzo was not there. He and his favored inner circle were spotted by chance in Mexico City, where an armed siege of their apartment ensued. Out of ammunition, Constanzo huddled in a closet with a male lover and ordered another gang member to shoot them both. 'Don't worry, I'll be back,' were his last words.

The rest were taken alive. In all, 14 cultists were given lengthy jail terms on charges from multiple murder to drug running. Oddest among them was Sara Aldrete, an all-American ex-college student from Brownsville, Texas, who had thrown away a glittering future as an athlete to join the cult. Sentenced in 1994 to 62 years without parole, she was asked why she had followed Constanzo. 'I could not leave him,' she said, 'because he threatened to use witchcraft on my family.'

Eric Cooke

To say that Eric Edgar Cooke had a bad start in life would be an understatement. Born in February 1931 in Perth, Western Australia, he suffered in childhood from his father's alcohol fueled beatings. Ostracized because of his harelip and cleft palate and resulting speech defect, Cooke grew up an angry, brooding loner.

Sad Childhood Of The Random Slayer

He took a succession of semi-skilled jobs, while committing a string of crimes in his neighborhood. After the accident-prone youth suffered several traumas to his head at work, he attempted to get his life together by enlisting in the military in 1952. He was discharged three months later when it was discovered that he had failed to declare a series of convictions for theft, breaking and entering, and arson of a church.

A year later, aged 22, Cooke again attempted to settle down by marrying Sarah Lavin, a 19-year-old waitress, and fathering seven children. Family life failed to calm him, however, and he continued to roam the streets by night, being arrested for minor offenses including voyeurism.

What turned Cooke from petty crime to serial killer is unclear but, in February 1959, he repeatedly and fatally stabbed an innocent woman while she was sleeping in her Perth apartment. Ten months later, armed with a knife and hatchet, he broke into the

home of a 22-year-old woman, hacking at her face after he delivered lethal stab wounds. The police discounted sex and robbery as motives, as the girls had not been raped and nothing had been stolen.

Cooke's subsequent killing spree involved a series of seemingly unrelated hit-and-runs, stabbings, stranglings, and shootings which held Perth in a grip of terror. This was a strangely inconsistent serial killer whose methods seemed as random as his choice of victims.

Victims had been shot with a variety of different rifles, stabbed with knives, scissors, and hit with an ax. One victim was shot dead after answering a knock on his door, several were killed upon waking while Cooke was robbing their homes. Two were shot while sleeping without their homes being disturbed. After stabbing one victim, he got lemonade from the refrigerator and sat on the porch drinking it.

In August 1963, an elderly couple gathering wildflowers near the Canning River found a rifle lying in the brush and called the police. Ballistics tests confirmed it was the weapon used to kill a babysitter a week earlier. The rifle was impounded, replaced with a lookalike, and detectives staked out the scene. They waited 15 days before Cooke arrived to claim the weapon, and he was taken into custody without a struggle.

Apart from the eight or more murders of which he was suspected, Cooke admitted having committed more than 200 thefts, five hit-and-run offenses against young women, and two murders for which other men had already been wrongly imprisoned. Evidence indeed pointed to Cooke being the killer of the two women, and the convictions against Darryl Beamish and John Button were quashed—but not before they had served a total of 20 years between them.

Despite Cooke's defense citing his disturbed childhood, head injuries, and spells in an asylum, the court rejected the claim that he suffered from schizophrenia. The state permitted no other psychiatric specialist to examine him and, in November 1963, he was convicted of wilful murder after a three-day trial in the Supreme Court of Western Australia.

Cooke was sentenced to death by hanging. He ordered his lawyers not to appeal, conceding that he deserved to pay for what he had done. Aged 33, Eric Cooke became the last person to be hanged at Fremantle Prison, on October 26, 1964.

Dean Corll

Dean Corll was known as 'The Candy Man' because of the years he had spent working at home with his mother, making candies and selling them in a small store attached to their house in Houston, Texas. He had always sought the company of young men but, during a spell in the US Army, he realized he was gay—and that his sexual urges could only be satisfied by inflicting pain.

The 'Candy Man' Who Hired Kids To Kill Kids

Released from service at the age of 25 in 1964, Corll returned to his job at the confectionary factory and tried to befriend boys by giving them sweets. At roughly the same time as complaints about his sexual advances became public, his mother closed the company and retired.

Her son moved to the suburb of Pasadena and became a trainee electrician for the Houston Lighting and Power Company. He was well liked by colleagues but some of them thought it strange that he spent his free time mixing only with young teenagers. Two of them became his particular friends: Elmer Henley and David Brooks, both of whom dropped out of high school to spend more time with Corll.

In fact, what they had embarked on was not merely a homosexual relationship with the older man but a murder spree of shocking savagery.

Corll had met Brooks when the schoolboy was only 12. The older man at first paid the boy for sexual favors but then enlisted him as an accomplice. Henley, by contrast, had originally been earmarked as one of Corll's victims but avoided death by his willingness to plumb any immoral depth—and that included delivering his best friends into Corll's clutches.

The mission of these two Houston youths was to cruise the area seeking boys with whom Corll could forcibly have sex. Operating mainly in the rundown Heights area, they found they had no problem persuading young drug addicts to go to Corll's home with the promise of wild parties. There they would suffer prolonged torture at the hands of Corll before being murdered. 'He killed them because he wanted to have sex and they didn't', Brooks later told police.

All the victims were young males between 13 and 20 years old. Corll's first known victim was 18-year-old Jeffrey Konen, a student of the University of Texas who vanished in September 1970 while hitch-hiking to his parents' Houston home.

Tragically, most of those who followed were even younger. Typical was Billy Ray Lawrence, a 15-year-old friend of Henley, who was kept alive by Corll for four days before he was killed. By that August 1973, when 13-year-old James Dreymala became Corll's last confirmed victim, the tally had reached at least 27, most of them procured by Brooks and Henley, who had graduated from simply supplying the victims to helping commit the occasional murder themselves.

The official list of Corll's victims is likely to be underestimated. Forty-two boys had vanished within the Houston area since 1970 but, despite the anxiety of parents over their missing sons, police had failed to come anywhere close to solving the mystery. To the frustration of the families, many of the disappearances were written down as 'runaways'.

The breakthrough, when it came, was not due to police diligence. At 3am on August 8, 1973, Henley turned up at Corll's home with one of his friends, Tim Kerley, who had been happy to accept an invitation to a glue sniffing party but was in fact the next intended victim. Henley had also brought along his girlfriend, 15-year-old Rhonda Williams.

Corll objected to the girl's presence and, while Henley and Williams were in a drug-induced stupor, handcuffed and bound them. The 17-year-old pleaded with Corll to untie him, promising to continue helping him carry out the night's planned murder. But as soon as his hands were freed, he grabbed his captor's gun and shot him six times at point-blank range. The reign of the 33-year-old mass killer was instantly ended.

Henley called the police who found that one of the bedrooms had been turned into a 'torture room'. The centerpiece was a thick board with shackles for hands and feet. Various instruments of torture, including an assortment of dildos, were in evidence. Police also noticed that many wall and floor surfaces were covered with plastic sheeting—the better to contain the bloodstains that nevertheless spattered some of the walls.

Forced to confess his part in procuring Corll's victims, Henley led police to a boatshed where 17 decomposing bodies of boys lay in shallow graves. Corll had spread lime around them to disguise the stench of decomposition. Next stop was a local tourist spot, Lake Sam Rayburn, where more naked corpses were unearthed.

Many of the bodies recovered showed signs of mutilation and torture. It appeared that one of Corll's perverted practices was to insert a glass rod into the urethra of a victim and break it. The total body count came to 27 but police believe the higher figure of 42 was more realistic.

Henley and Brooks were tried in 1974 at San Antonio, where their pleas of insanity were rejected. Henley was found guilty of nine murders and sentenced to 594 years in prison. Brooks got life after being found guilty of one murder.

Juan Corona

Juan Vallejo Corona was at one time labeled the worst and most notorious mass murderer in United States history. Sadly, his tally of 25, killed during just a few months of 1971, did not remain a record for long. The other tragedy was that, by the nature of his crimes, many of the victims were barely missed. They were mostly Mexican migrants, largely itinerant fruit pickers, who hardly mixed with the local rural populations of California's Sutter County and of Feather River, where most of the killings took place.

Killer Dug Graves To Await Victims

Corona, born in 1933, had been an itinerant himself, having crossed the border into California as a 16-year-old in 1950. Despite his lack of schooling, he steadily worked his way up to become a successful businessman, a licensed labor contractor in charge of hiring fellow migrant workers to pick the fruit crops of the Yuba City area.

His book-keeping was meticulous—as police discovered when they followed up an anonymous tip and raided his farmhouse, near Feather River, in 1971. There they found 25 names carefully listed in a ledger. They corresponded with Mexican migrants and other itinerants all of whom had disappeared in the previous few months. Their bodies had been secreted around the farmstead after being hacked to death with knives and machetes.

The alarm had been raised on May 19, when a local rancher noticed that a hole, the size of a grave, had been dug in his peach orchard. Returning there the next day, he saw that it had been filled in with freshly dug earth. When police investigated, they unearthed the body of Kenneth Whitacre, a 40-year-old vagrant, who had been sodomized, stabbed to death, and his head almost severed with a machete.

The gruesome discovery sparked off the hunt for more buried bodies, with 25 eventually being found, although police maintained there must have been many more. The victims had all been murdered during a period of six weeks; an average of one death every 40 hours.

One grave alone yielded nine bodies. All had been subjected to homosexual rape before being stabbed and viciously slashed around the head. Corona had buried them face up, with their arms stretched above their heads and their shirts pulled up over their faces. Some had their pants pulled down.

When police searched Corona's farmhouse, they found—in addition to the notebook—a machete, a pistol, two butcher's knives, and bloodstained clothes. It became obvious that he had carefully planned the killings—digging a fresh grave in advance of each attack.

At his trial in 1973, his lawyers argued that all 25 charges of murder should be dismissed on the grounds of their client's mental instability. He had twice been treated at a psychiatric hospital where he had been diagnosed with paranoid schizophrenia, they argued. But their pleas were ignored and Corona was given 25 life sentences.

The killer lodged further failed legal appeals over the years, once telling a prison doctor: 'Yes, I did it but I'm a sick man and can't be judged by the standards of other men.'

During a parole bid in 2003, by which time he was 69, he said: 'The victims were all people who didn't have a family and they were ready to go to the next world.'

Mary Ann Cotton

Unlike most serial killers, Mary Ann Cotton was on intimate terms with all of her victims. The reason was clear, for all were members of her immediate family. It is not known exactly how many people she murdered but the candidates include her mother, three of her four husbands (one of them being bigamous), a lover, her best friend, plus 15 children, including 10 from among her own brood of 12.

Churchgoer Commits Multiple Murders With Arsenic

That was a British serial-killing record that has survived well over a century—and all the more remarkable since Mary Ann was a churchgoing girl born in 1832 far from the lure of any big city. Raised by strict Methodist parents in the County Durham mining village of Low Moorsley, Mary Ann was married in 1852 at the age of 20 to William Mowbray. They had eight children but the family appeared to be

ABOVE: Mary Ann Cotton, the churchgoer who claimed around 20 victims through arsenic poisoning in the 19th century.

James Robinson, asked Mary Ann to marry him. Conveniently, mother was dead within 10 days. Mary Ann herself became mother to James Robinson's five children, taking with her the surviving daughter Isabella. Within a few short months Isabella and four of the Robinson children had died from supposed natural causes. Robinson left his wife, taking with him his remaining child, and in doing so became the only husband to survive.

Mary Ann did not stay single for long, however. Even though she was still legally married, she next wed Frederick Cotton, who had two children from a previous marriage. Mary Ann soon fell pregnant and had another child but a year into the marriage, Frederick Cotton was also dead. Gastric fever was blamed.

At this juncture in her killing spree, Mary Ann met up with a former lover, Joseph Nattrass. The resumed romance was ill-fated, however, as the greedy widow found yet another way of improving her lifestyle. This time her heart was set on a customs officer by the name of Mr Quick-Manning and poor Joseph Nattrass was suddenly dispensable. Mary Ann killed him, along with her stepsons from her bigamous marriage to Cotton: 10-year-old Frederick junior and 14-month-old baby Charlie.

It was this final murder that doomed Mary Ann Cotton. Little Charlie had been fine one day and dead the next. His tiny body was subjected to an autopsy, which revealed not only the cause of his early demise— arsenic poisoning—but also the probable cause of all the other family deaths.

The suspicion was confirmed when the bodies of other family members were exhumed, and 40-year-old Mary Ann Cotton was tried for murder at Durham Assizes on March 5, 1873. Justice was swift and two weeks later she walked from her cell to the gallows.

plagued by health problems. One by one, the brothers, sisters, and their father William himself all died of gastric fevers. In fact she had poisoned them. Only one among the family survived, a daughter named Isabella who had been sent away to live with her grandmother.

Following the death of her poor husband, Mary Ann married George Ward. Yet after only 13 months he too was dead. The widow even murdered her own mother, who became ill at the same time as her third husband,

Thomas Cream

Dr Thomas Neill Cream stood with a hood over his head and a noose around his neck on the scaffold at London's Newgate Prison in 1892 and, so the story goes, declared: 'I am Jack the...' He was cut short when the trap door burst open beneath his feet and he was hanged.

Last Boast Of The 'Lambeth Poisoner'

Cream, tagged the 'Lambeth Poisoner', had initially been a suspect in the search for Jack the Ripper, the killer of five women in London at the close of the 19th century (see page 95). But since he could prove that he was in jail in America at the time the Ripper was operating, his cry was judged a final attempt at a dramatic exit.

Cream was born in Glasgow in May 1850 to parents who emigrated to Canada, where the studious young

ABOVE: Strychnine was the method of execution favored by the 'Lambeth Poisoner', Dr Thomas Cream.

Thomas qualified as a doctor. In 1876 he married Flora Brooks in a shotgun wedding—after her parents discovered he had carried out a bungled abortion on her that left her seriously ill. The day after the nuptials, however, Cream abandoned his wife, who later died—possibly at Cream's hands.

The callous doctor fled to Britain where he continued his medical studies in London and Edinburgh before returning to Canada and setting up a practice in London, Ontario. Soon afterward, in August 1879, the body of a woman was found in an alley near his surgery. She had earlier visited Cream to seek an abortion.

Under suspicion, Cream moved to Chicago, where he specialized in offering abortions to prostitutes. When one of his patients died in August 1880, he was taken into custody but released for lack of evidence.

Cream was again arrested a year later when the husband of one of his patients died of strychnine poisoning. There was firm evidence that Cream had supplied the wife with the poison, but when she turned state's evidence, the doctor was left to face a murder charge alone. He was sentenced to life in November 1881.

With remission, Cream was released a decade later and, with an inheritance left him by his father, returned to England and settled in Lambeth, a working-class area of Victorian London rife with crime and prostitution. In October 1891, he picked up two prostitutes, aged 19 and 27, both of whom died of strychnine poisoning.

The following April, he offered a girl some pills that he said would help clear a rash on her face. Suspicious because of her client's insistence that she swallow them all, she merely pretended to do so, thereby saving herself from the 'Lambeth Poisoner'.

But two other prostitutes hired by Cream a week later were not so fortunate. The girls, aged 18 and 21, were offered drinks the killer had brought with him and both died in agony. At last, suspicion fell on the local doctor, who was arrested at his home in June 1892. Police found seven bottles of strychnine in his rooms.

At the Old Bailey, Cream's pleas of innocence were rejected, the jury taking just 10 minutes to decide he was guilty. Seeming surprised at the verdict, he strutted from the dock, defiantly stating: 'They shall never hang me.' He was proved wrong on the morning of November 15, 1892.

Alexander Pichushkin

Alexander Yuryevich Pichushkin lured his victims to Moscow's vast, wooded Bitsevsky Park with the promise of a bottle of beer or a shot of vodka. Occasionally, he would suggest a game of chess. And after bludgeoning each victim to death, he would place a coin or vodka bottle stopper on one more square on the chessboard in his apartment. That is the way the notorious serial killer recorded his grisly crimes, attaching a number to another square of the board every time he struck. By the time he was caught, Pichushkin had filled in 62 of the 64 squares.

Woodland Victims Drowned In A Pit Of Filth

The 'Chessboard Killer', as Pichushkin came to be known, first struck in 1992 when he was just 18 years old, murdering the boyfriend of a neighbor he had fallen in love with. He later killed the girl, whose body

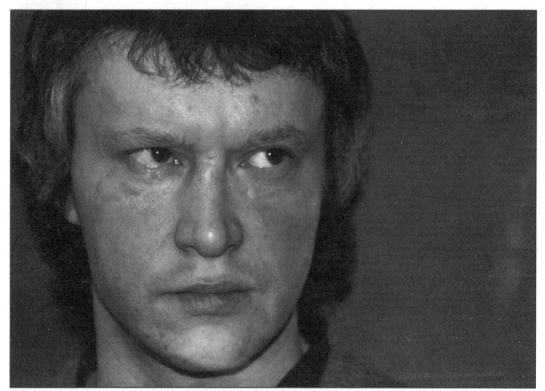

ABOVE: At one point during 2005, Alexander Pichushkin, 'The Chessboard Killer', was committing one murder a week.

was found in Bitsevsky Park, near to the apartment block where Pichushkin lived with his aged mother.

Subsequent murders were sporadic but in 2005 the supermarket shelf-stacker embarked on a killing spree. At one stage, police were uncovering one body every week—all having the serial killer's hallmark of a smashed skull, with the neck of a vodka bottle thrust into the gaping wound.

Most of his victims were homeless drifters or drunks. Those who were not killed instantly ended their agonies by drowning after Pichushkin threw them into the sewers that ran beneath the park. Others were strangled or killed with a blow to the skull from a hammer or blunt object. He would always attack from behind in order to stop blood from soaking his clothes, and finally he would stick the neck of a vodka bottle into his victims' skull, ensuring that they did not survive.

Three of his victims were women and one a child, a homeless nine-year-old boy. The body of one woman was found with tiny stakes hammered into her skull and around her eyes. His final victim, a female colleague from the supermarket where he worked, caused Pichushkin's capture. Before accompanying the killer to the park, she had left a note with her son telling her who she was meeting. CCTV cameras also caught them strolling toward the park shortly before she was murdered there in June 2006.

Under arrest, 32-year-old Pichushkin confessed: 'I liked to watch their agony. For me, a life without murder is like a life without food for anyone else. I felt like the father of all these people, since it was I who opened the door for them to another world.'

A psychologist who analyzed the killer prior to his trial in September 2007 reported that his love of chess, which ironically he couldn't play, was a clue to his character. Pichushkin, it was said, 'is detached from human beings, who are no more than wooden dolls—like chess pieces to him'.

At his trial, the prosecution claimed that Pichushkin 'dreamed of going down in history by surpassing Andrei Chikatilo'—the so-called 'Rostov Ripper' who was Russia's previously most notorious serial killer, executed in 1994 for murdering 52 women and children (see page 43). Pichushkin wished to confess to 62 slayings but there was sufficient evidence for only 48

ABOVE: The 'Bitsevsky Maniac' is escorted into the Moscow City Court on August 13, 2007.

charges of murder. With the death penalty no longer in force, he was jailed for life, with the first 15 years in solitary confinement.

Jerry Brudos

A detective asked Jerry Brudos a simple question: 'Do you feel some remorse, Jerry? Do you feel sorry for your victims, for the girls who died?' Brudos picked up a piece of paper, screwed it up and threw it on the floor. 'That much,' he said. 'I care about those girls as much as that piece of wadded up paper...'

Fetish Fiend Dressed Dead Bodies Like Dolls

Jerome Henry Brudos was a murdering rapist with a fetish for women's clothes and shoes. He first came to police attention when, as a 17-year-old, he forced a woman to pose for naked pictures at knifepoint. He was confined to a mental hospital for nine months with a personality disorder.

After his release, he continued stealing underwear from washing lines. By the time he was 28 and committed his first murder, Brudos had accumulated a large collection of women's attire.

That first victim was a 19-year-old encyclopedia saleswoman, Linda Slawson, who knocked on the door of the Brudos home in Portland, Oregon, one day in January 1968. With his wife and two children upstairs, Brudos, then aged 28, knocked the young woman unconscious.

He took Linda to the garage where he strangled her and abused the corpse. Brudos then sent his family out for hamburgers so he could play with her body. He dressed her up like a doll in the clothes he had been collecting over the years and photographed his handiwork. Finally, he chopped off the left foot and, with a newly fitted shoe, put it in his refrigerator. The body was disposed of in the Willamette River.

Three other murders followed. Jan Whitney, 23, was picked up at the roadside in November 1968 when her car broke down. He took her home and raped the corpse. After dressing her up, he decided to keep her and hung her from a hook in the garage ceiling. Several days later he consigned her body to the river, but not before slicing off her right breast.

ABOVE: The Willamette River in Portland, Oregon, where Jerry Brudos dumped the bodies of most of his victims.

Student Karen Sprinkler, 19, was abducted from a department store car park in March 1969 and taken to his home, where she was forced to pose for him. She was then hanged and her body similarly abused. This time, both breasts were removed before her corpse was dumped, this time in the Long Tom River.

Linda Salee, 23, died a month later. Brudos had flashed a fake police badge at her and 'arrested' her for shoplifting. He took her back to the garage where he strangled and raped her as she expired. He kept the body for a day, violating the corpse before she too ended up in the river.

After quizzing fellow students of Karen Sprinkler, police discovered several girls had received phone calls from a man asking to meet them. A trap was set with one of the girls arranging a date with Brudos and he was arrested.

He pleaded insanity at his trial but psychiatric reports declared him sane. He was sentenced to life imprisonment at Oregon State Penitentiary.

Peter Sutcliffe

The hunt for the 'Yorkshire Ripper' began with the grisly discovery of the half-naked and viciously stabbed body of 28-year-old prostitute Wilma McCann on a Leeds playing field on the morning of October 30, 1975. The manhunt, dogged by blunders and slip-ups, lasted five years until, 13 murders and seven attempted murders later, Peter William Sutcliffe was finally caught in a routine motoring check. In his car, he had the luckiest prostitute in Yorkshire, along with a Phillips screwdriver and a ball-peen hammer.

Police Blunders Left 'Yorkshire Ripper' Free To Kill

Following the **Wilma McCann killing,** Sutcliffe's next target was prostitute Emily Jackson, 42, whose body was found in the Chapeltown red-light district of

ABOVE: A phototfit image of the man Yorkshire police failed to capture for five years.

ABOVE: Peter Sutcliffe on his wedding day in August 1974. He began murdering women a year later.

ABOVE: Six of the Yorkshire Ripper's victims. Top left to right; Vera Millward, Jayne MacDonald, and Josephine Whittaker. Bottom left to right; Jean Royle, Helga Rytka, and Barbara Leach.

Leeds. Her post-mortem revealed more than 50 stab wounds inflicted with a Phillips screwdriver, the imprint of a size-seven Dunlop boot on her thigh and two heavy blows with a hammer to her head, the cause of her death.

Prostitute Number Three was also attacked with a hammer and, having masturbated over her semi-conscious body, Sutcliffe left her with £5 and a warning not to tell. Her description was found to be very accurate but, in a series of police errors, was largely ignored.

His next three victims in 1977 all bore similar horrific injuries: bodies face down, hammer blows to the skull, and frenzied stabbing to the stomach. Victim Number Seven in July that year survived the Ripper's attack and, following emergency surgery, was able to give a poor description.

The Ripper knew the police were scouring Leeds and Bradford and so found new hunting grounds. In October he murdered Jean Jordan, a 21-year-old prostitute in Manchester. Her body lay undetected for over a week, but he left a vital clue: a brand new £5 note, which had been issued to only 6,000 employees,

ABOVE: The bus stop outside the Arndale shopping center in Leeds, where Jacqueline Hill was last seen alive.

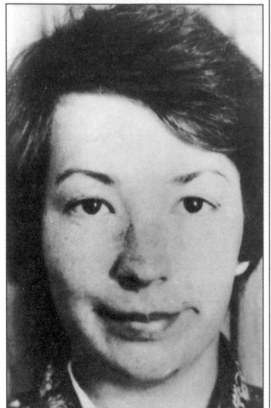

ABOVE: Student Jacqueline Hill, 20, was the Ripper's 13th and final victim, murdered in Leeds in November 1980.

among them those of the firm that employed Sutcliffe as a lorry driver. He was interviewed but police failed to pick up on his criminal record, which recorded his arrest in 1969 for 'going equipped for theft' with a hammer.

Following his next attack, in December that year—during which he screamed, 'You dirty prostitute' at his surviving victim—Sutcliffe killed again twice in 10 days. He hammered and stabbed Yvonne Pearson to death in January 1978, returning to her body before its discovery some two months later to inflict more macabre wounds. His next victim, an 18-year-old, was the only one he had sex with. Three more killings followed that summer, all victims receiving similar horrific wounds, including savage hammer blows to the head and the slashing to the stomach.

ABOVE: Yorkshire police chiefs look satisfied with Sutcliffe's conviction. But for their blunders, he would have been stopped sooner.

Sutcliffe lay low for almost a year without any further murders. More than 250 officers were working full-time to try and catch him, their attempts plagued by hoaxes. The police concentrated on suspects with Geordie accents following an audio tape supposedly from the Ripper.

With his final two victims, Sutcliffe changed his modus operandi in a bid to throw police off the scent. The second of these was lucky; a passing police car

LEFT: Police hold back crowds outside Dewsbury court during an appearance by Sutcliffe on murder chages in January 1981.

disturbed Sutcliffe. A 20-year-old student from Leeds was not so lucky, however, and became his next murder victim in November 1980.

Up until the time of his capture, Sutcliffe had been interviewed five times by police. He was known to frequent red-light districts. He had a previous record for possession of a hammer. Yet, as he didn't have a Geordie accent, he was never marked as a prime suspect.

Following his confession, Sutcliffe was tried at the Old Bailey and, on May 22, 1981, was sentenced to life, with a recommendation that he serve at least 30 years. Since then, he has been held in Broadmoor Hospital for the criminally insane. The reason for his crimes? According to his brother Carl, Peter Sutcliffe felt he was just 'cleaning up the streets'.

RIGHT: Multiple killer Peter Sutcliffe is bundled into Dewsbury court under a blanket on January 6, 1981.

Joseph Swango

Born Joseph Michael Swango, he shone at school, studying music and then biology before going on to Southern Illinois University where he graduated in medicine in 1983, at the age of 28, winning a year-long internship in general surgery at the Ohio State University Medical Center. But in January 1984, it was first noted that the former prize pupil was acting suspiciously. A nurse saw him checking on a patient and shortly afterward found the woman turning blue and suffocating. Emergency treatment managed to save her but a week later she was dead. Swango had been the last person to attend to her.

How Many Did The 'Doughnut Poisoner' Murder?

Similar occurrences rang alarm bells with anxious nurses who, comparing notes, discovered that at least six other patients, all evidently making good progress, had suddenly died. Their ages ranged from 19 to 47. Swango had been the duty intern at the time each of them had succumbed. Incredibly, although an investigation was carried out, none of the nurses who had raised the alarm were interviewed.

The high number of deaths whenever Swango was around continued, however, and the hospital terminated his employment. Swango returned to his hometown of Quincy, Illinois, where he joined the Adams County Ambulance Corps. On one occasion, an entire paramedic crew became ill after eating doughnuts bought in by Swango. His colleagues decided to investigate the newcomer a little further—and found arsenic in his locker. When alerted, police searched the poisoner's apartment and discovered a hoard of phials, bottles, syringes, and a library of books on murder. There was also a selection of guns and knives.

Dubbed the 'Doughnut Poisoner', Swango was arrested and charged with seven counts of aggravated battery. In April 1985, a court sentenced him to five years' imprisonment. He was released for good behavior only two years later.

Happily for hospital staff and patients, Joseph Swango spent the next few years in various jobs away from medicine. He also had a girlfriend, Kirstin Kinney, a 26-

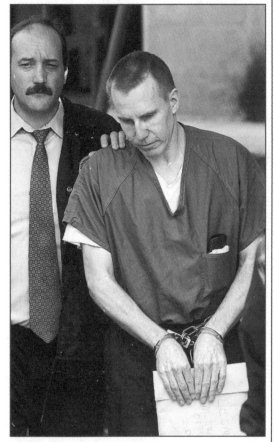

ABOVE: Justice finally caught up with Joseph Swango in July 2000 when he pleaded guilty to four murders.

year-old nurse who moved with him to South Dakota in 1992 when Swango accepted a position as emergency doctor at the Veterans Affairs Medical Center in Sioux Falls. Both he and Kirstin were considered dedicated staffers.

The love affair ended, however, when a program about the notorious 'Doughnut Poisoner' was shown on television. Swango was dismissed. Kirstin, who realized the migraine headaches she now repeatedly suffered seemed to disappear whenever she was away from her boyfriend, fled home, wrote a note to her parents and shot herself.

With the fake references that he had become expert in forging, Swango moved to New York State in 1993 and got a job at the Internal Medicine Department at the Veterans Administration Headquarters, Northport, Long Island. His first patient died within hours of his arrival. Others were also to die in his 'care', all suffering heart failure in the dead of night.

It was not good police work or the vigilance of hospital authorities that finally halted Swango but Kirstin Kinney's parents, who could not forgive him for driving their daughter to suicide. They alerted the Long Island hospital and he was fired, the hospital authorities writing to every medical school in America warning them about him.

Swango disappeared, surfacing again in Zimbabwe at the Mnene Lutheran Outpost Hospital—where patients started to die with alarming regularity. A police investigation was launched and Swango fled to neighboring Zambia, and finally back to America. He was arrested the moment he landed at Chicago's O'Hare Airport in June 1997. He was finally charged with four counts of murder, pleaded guilty and, in July 2000, was sentenced to life imprisonment without parole.

Although only ever convicted of four murders, Swango is suspected of many more, estimates ranging from 35 to 60 in the United States—and perhaps hundreds overseas. A statement issued at the time by the mass poisoner's *alma mater*, Southern Illinois University, read: 'If Swango is legally connected to all the suspicious deaths of patients under his care since he began his residency with Ohio State University's medical program in 1983, it would make him the most prolific serial killer in history'.

Johann Unterweger

The most extraordinary thing about Johann 'Jack' Unterweger was that anyone believed him. When he was arrested for the murder of a teenaged girl, he seemed to be just another one-off killer. By the time he had reinvented himself as a 'reformed' celebrity ex-criminal, he had killed at least 11.

The Killer Who Became A TV Celebrity

Unterweger was born in Styria, southeastern Austria, in 1951 to a local prostitute and an American soldier he never knew. He was raised in the company of streetwalkers, their pimps and assorted petty thieves. He spent most of his late teens and early 20s in prison. By the age of 25, he had notched up 15 convictions, including burglary, rape, and pimping. So when, in 1975, he was convicted of strangling an 18-year-old girl with her own bra, the life sentence he received should have removed him from public harm forever.

While inside, however, he wrote poetry, a novel, and an autobiography titled *Fegefeuer* (Purgatory), which became a bestseller. His writing was unexpectedly proficient, and he achieved celebrity status, with a clutch of literary awards. Suddenly infamy turned to fame, and a petition organized by influential Austrians in the literary world helped him gain early release from prison in October 1990.

Unterweger was feted at glitterati events and on TV chat shows. He became a journalist, presenting himself as a reformed character and explaining away his violent past and rehabilitated future: 'I was no longer a youth. I was a beast, a devil, a child grown old before his time who enjoyed being evil. But that life is now over. Let's get on with the new.'

But Unterweger had fooled an entire nation. Within months of his release, he started killing again. During his first year of freedom, he is reckoned to have strangled at least six prostitutes. As more bodies turned up, it was only natural for the media to seek an expert on the subject— and, bizarrely, Unterweger found himself being asked for his opinions and advice on the latest deaths for which he alone was responsible. The killer basked in the spotlight while watching his books rise up the bestsellers list.

The only people not fooled were the police. They were suspicious of the publicity-seeking ex-jailbird and began linking the new slayings to Unterweger's movements. The killing spree spread across the Austrian countryside and into neighboring Czechoslovakia. Unterweger killed six women in the spring of 1991, the bodies of four victims who had vanished from the streets of Vienna being found during April and May alone.

The killings stopped in Austria shortly afterward— and began in Los Angeles. That was because Unterweger had been commissioned by a Vienna magazine to write an article on crime in Southern California. There, while asking the LA police to assist him with his research, he committed three murders in June and July, all of prostitutes whom he strangled with their own bras, afterward violating their battered bodies with sticks and other objects.

Unterweger was arrested in February 1992 in Florida, where he was traveling with his 18-year-old girlfriend. After a legal battle over whether he should be tried in the United States or Europe, he was extradited to Austria where he finally stood trial in April 1994. A psychologist described him in court as: 'A sexually sadistic psychopath with narcissistic and histrionic tendencies, prone to fits of rage and anger. He is an incorrigible perpetrator.'

Accused of 11 murder charges, including the three American cases, Unterweger was convicted of nine of them, two bodies being too decomposed for cause of death to be determined. On June 29, 1994, he was sentenced to life without parole and was taken to Graz prison where, just 12 hours later, he hanged himself in his cell using his own clothes as a noose—exactly as he had killed most of his victims.

John Haigh

John Haigh relished the title bestowed on him by the press: 'The Acid Bath Murderer'. He used industrial acid to dissolve away evidence of his crimes and, but for one careless oversight, would almost certainly have gone on to claim the lives of many more victims. It was his mistaken belief that a corpse could be completely disposed of by chemicals that led him to the gallows in 1949.

Deadly Charm Of The 'Acid Bath Murderer'

J ohn George Haigh was a charmer. Born in 1909 and raised in a Yorkshire village by parents who were strict followers of the Plymouth Brethren sect, he grew up a bright scholarship pupil and choirboy. But when, at the age of 21, he was fired from an early job for

ABOVE: Dr Archibald Henderson and his wife Rose on holiday in 1944. They were both killed by the Acid Bath Murderer.

ABOVE: Haigh arrives at Horsham Magistrates Court handcuffed to a policeman, on April 1, 1949.

draft dodger named Donald McSwann, was killed there in September 1944, Haigh smashing his skull with a pin-table leg and dissolving his body in a 40-gallon (180 liters) water butt filled with sulphuric acid. The little that was left of McSwann was then poured down a drain.

Haigh contacted the young man's parents, wealthy

ABOVE: Haigh's vile crimes make the front page of the *Daily Express* newspaper on March 3, 1949.

stealing cash, he turned his hand to forgery and fraud, specializing in selling cars he didn't own. As the cash rolled in, Haigh acquired a gleaming sports car and a pretty wife. He lost both when he was jailed for fraud in 1934 and again in 1938.

Incarcerated in bleak Dartmoor prison, Haigh studied chemistry and worked in the tinsmith's store where he had access to sulphuric acid. The idea of dissolving bodies in acid began to take shape. He experimented on small animals brought in as pets by prisoners on outside work parties. He made careful notes about the time taken for acid to dissolve flesh and bone.

Freed in 1944, Haigh moved to the capital and set up his own business repairing pin-tables in basement rooms in London's Gloucester Road. His first murder victim, a

ABOVE: Rose Henderson in 1945. After murdering Rose and her husband, Haigh used forged papers to embezzle £7,000.

businessman William and wife Amy, with a message that their son had gone into hiding to avoid his call-up papers. When they turned up to learn more, they too were murdered and their remains swilled down the drain. Using forged papers, Haigh seized control of £4,000 of their assets and moved into the nearby Onslow Court Hotel. With money came a passion for gambling, however, and Haigh's debts mounted. He decided that new victims were needed.

The killer had moved his repair workshop to Crawley, Sussex, where, in February 1948, he lured London doctor Archibald Henderson and his wife Rose, murdered them and consigned their bodies to the acid vat. After forging letters giving him authority over their assets, he embezzled £7,000.

Haigh's final victim was a fellow resident of the Onslow Court Hotel, 69-year-old colonel's widow Olive Durand-Deacon. Lured to Crawley in February 1949, she was shot in the back and heaved into the acid vat. The resultant gunge was then poured onto the earth at the back of the workshop. Haigh had been too hasty, however. When police arrived, at the behest of a friend of the victim who knew of her appointment with Haigh, they found bone and false teeth which the acid had failed to dissolve.

Although police suspected Haigh of up to 15 murders, he confessed to just six. A jury at Lewes Assizes took just 17 minutes to declare him guilty. The deadly charming con-man was hanged at London's Wandsworth prison on August 10, 1949.

ABOVE: A crowd gathers outside Wandsworth prison in anticipation of news of Haigh's hanging.

Henri Landru

Henri Landru was born in 1869 to a poor but honest hardworking couple. They gave him the middle name Desiré, meaning much desired. And indeed, despite his small stature, Landru would in time prove to be a magnet for the opposite sex. Given the nickname 'Bluebeard', he preyed on the women of Paris during World War One while their menfolk were away fighting—and it cost at least 11 of the ladies their lives.

French 'Bluebeard' Was A Ladykiller

ABOVE: Henri Landru pleads his innocence from the witness box during his trial in November 1921.

Landru married in 1893 and had three children but he gave up his job as an architect's clerk to lead a life of petty crime. On the run from the law, he started advertising for a new wife, even though he was still married. A widow aged 39, Jeanne Cuchet answered him and was greatly impressed by 'the widower Monsieur Diard', as Landru was calling himself. In December 1914, she gave up her apartment and, with her son, moved in with 'Diard' at his rented villa outside Paris.

Mme Cuchet and her son then vanished without trace, leaving Landru in possession of 15,000 francs worth of jewels, furniture, and securities. Over the next five years, Landru entertained scores of other women, at least 10 of whom never returned home. They ranged from a 19-year-old serving girl to a 44-year-old widow pretending to be aged 29.

Alarmed relatives began contacting the local mayor seeking help in tracing their loved ones. When he put

ABOVE: Two guards stand next to the oven in which Landru burned the bodies of his many victims.

ABOVE: 'Bluebeard', the murderous womanizer and nine of the victims he killed for money.

An arrest warrant was issued and, in April 1919, Landru was spotted strolling down a Paris street arm in arm with his proposed next victim. Police searched his city lodgings and recovered a handwritten book meticulously recording the women he had met through his advertisements, together with an account of their riches. A search of his country villa revealed the cause of thick, black, oily smoke that neighbors had noticed emitting from the chimney. Almost 300 fragments of bones and teeth were recovered from the stove where Landru had burned the dismembered bodies.

them in touch with one another, the families realized that the common factor in the disappearances was the bearded charmer, now confusingly going under the various names 'Fremyet', 'Cuchet', 'Guillet', 'Dupont', and 'Diard'.

ABOVE: The courtroom at Seine-et-Oise during Landru's trial. He was found guilty and sentenced to death in November 1921.

ABOVE: Landru burned the bodies of his victims in a stove in this house, pictured here in 1921.

Landru vehemently denied all charges, so there was never an answer to the question of how many victims he had claimed—many more than the 11 known about, it was suspected. At his trial at Seine-et-Oise court in November 1921, he was found guilty and, to hysterical scenes inside and outside the courtroom, was sentenced to die.

He faced his death, at Versailles prison in February 1922, like the gentleman he pretended to be. He refused the priest's offer of a confession, and instead wrote a note to the chief prosecutor at his trial: 'Farewell Monsieur. Our common history will doubtless die tomorrow. I will die with an innocent and quiet mind. I hope, respectfully, that you may do the same.' The next morning, after persuading the warders not to shave off his beard, Landru's shirt was ripped open and his neck laid on the guillotine. His last words were: 'I shall be brave'.

ABOVE: An artist sketches the scene of one of Landru's murders, in 1921.

Bobby Joe Long

Who knows what goes on in a brain as severely traumatized as that of Bobby Joe Long? He could not understand the forces that drove him to rape more than 50 women; neither could he control them. He was utterly disgusted with what he was doing but could not stop. And when his sexual obsession turned to murder, he knew that he just had to get himself caught.

The Serial Rapist Who Wanted To Get Caught

Robert Joe Long, born 1953 in Kenova, West Virginia, was the product of a broken home and was completely dominated by his mother, who was constantly on the move seeking new jobs and new partners. At the age of 11, he was struck by a congenital disorder which caused his glands to produce extra oestrogen, making him grow breasts. Surgeons had to remove tissue from his chest but, although the physical abnormality was largely fixed, he was mentally scarred by the experience.

At 19, Long enlisted in the Army and six months later married his childhood sweetheart, who by all accounts was as dominant as his mother. At 20, he suffered a fractured skull in a motorcycle crash that left him in a coma for weeks. When he came round, he found that the least annoyance would make him erupt in violence. It was also, he said, when his uncontrollable sexual fixations began.

He demanded sex from his wife at least twice a day and masturbated obsessively. As a result, she divorced him and left with their two children. Sex also dominated his working day. He was a hospital X-ray technician but was fired from several posts for propositioning female patients, for showing a young girl pornographic pictures, and for ordering women to undress unnecessarily.

In 1976, he began raping regularly. Operating in and around Miami, Fort Lauderdale, and Ocala, Florida, he earned the nickname 'The Classified Ad Rapist' by ringing numbers from newspaper adverts and making appointments with housewives alone during daytime. Having gained entry to their homes, he would pull a knife, tie the victim up, and rape her.

From 1983, Long began murdering the women he abducted. At first in Jacksonville and then in the Tampa Bay area, he would cruise around looking for prostitutes or pick them up in seedy bars. He would take them to his apartment, bind them with rope and neck ligatures, then strangle them, bludgeon them or cut their throats. The bodies would be dumped, displayed in crude postures. During an eight-month period, he murdered at least nine women in the Tampa Bay area alone.

Long finally allowed himself to be caught by freeing one of his last victims, a 17-year-old girl whom he pounced on in November 1984 as she cycled home from her night-shift job at a bakery. He drove around with her blindfolded in his car for 26 hours and, although he raped her, he did not kill her. 'I knew when I let her go that it would only be a matter of time,' he said later. 'I just didn't care any more. I wanted to stop. I was sick inside.'

Nevertheless, two days later he struck again, strangling his final victim and driving around with her naked body but, on this one occasion, failing to rape her. Four days later, police identified him from the evidence of the freed 17-year-old. The following year, Long was found guilty of nine murders and given 32 life sentences and one death sentence.

He stalled all of the state's efforts to send him to Florida's electric chair, however, successfully gaining two new trials in one of the killings, though he was found guilty and re-sentenced to death both times. He was still sitting on Death Row two decades after his arrest.

A clue as to what made Bobby Joe Long tick came in a prison interview he gave. Talking of a stripper who accosted him up in a bar, he said he killed her because he was revolted by her. 'She picked me up,' he said. 'I didn't go after her. She was a whore. She manipulated men and she wanted to manipulate me. Once I had her in the car, I tied her up and raped her. Then I dumped her body along the highway. Next morning I couldn't believe what I had done. I was sick. Then I met another girl…and it happened all over again.'

Pedro López

Pedro López explained his murderous ways to police thus: 'I lost my innocence at the age of eight—so I decided to do the same to as many young girls as I could.' Born to a penniless prostitute in Tolmia, Colombia, in 1949, Pedro was one of 13 children. When the eight-year-old was caught sexually molesting one of his sisters, his mother threw him out of the house.

Did 'Monster Of The Andes' Kill 300?

Left to beg and steal on the streets, López was himself molested by a man who pretended to befriend him. At 18, he was jailed for auto theft and, on his second day in jail was gang-raped by fellow inmates. He got his revenge by murdering three of them with a knife he had fashioned—a revenge that cost him another two years behind bars after he pleaded that he had acted in self defense.

By the time he was finally freed, López was a hardened criminal and a killer beyond compare in South American criminal history. He earned himself the title 'Monster of the Andes', eventually confessing

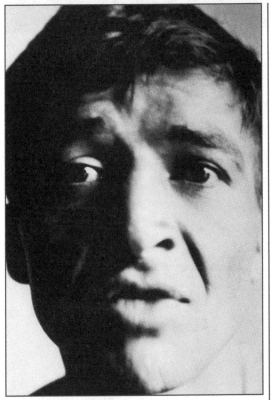

ABOVE: Vile Pedro López liked to see his victims' faces as they were murdered, so he always operated during daylight hours.

April 1980 when a flash flood near Ambato, Ecuador, almost 10,000ft (3,000m) up in the Andes, unearthed the remains of some of his victims. Days later, López was caught by townspeople while trying to abduct a 12-year-old girl from a marketplace. Under arrest, he refused to answer questions, so police used an old ploy to trick him. They placed a priest in the same cell posing as a prisoner. The ruse worked almost too well. López confessed to such revolting acts of sadistic violence that the priest asked to be removed.

Confronted with the evidence, López finally cracked. He told of his five years as the 'Monster of the Andes', relating countless abductions of young girls, whom he would rape and then strangle while staring eagerly into their eyes. He said watching their death throes gave him heightened sexual pleasure.

López confessed to killing as many as 110 girls in Ecuador, 100 in Colombia, and 'many more than 100' in Peru. His story was only fully believed when he led police to his 'killing fields'. Near Ambato, mass graves held 53 girls aged between eight and 12. Police unearthed 28 other graveyards, although in many cases they had already been disturbed by wild animals.

Lopez was given a life sentence, segregated from other prisoners at Ambato prison following threats to castrate him and burn him alive. Prison director Major Victor Lascano said: 'We may never know how many young girls Lopez killed. His estimate of 300 may even be too low.'

to the murder of 300 girls and, for a while, winning notoriety as the world's worst serial killer.

Roaming the impoverished countryside, his early victims were members of the native Indian tribes living on either side of the borders with neighboring Peru and Ecuador. López would stalk his young victims, sometimes for days, before approaching them with a supposed message from their mothers. López would then lead the girls to the outskirts of town where he would rape and kill them. He never worked at night because, as he later explained, he wanted to see his victim's face as she was murdered.

The hunt for a mass murderer began in earnest in

ABOVE: López during police interrogation in April 1980. He eventually confessed all to a priest, who was posing as a prisoner.

Charles Manson

By the age of 32, Charles Manson was so institutionalized, having spent most of his life in prison, that he pleaded to stay in jail. If only the authorities had granted his wish. Two years later he had gathered a cult of impressionable devotees who were willing to kill to stay in his evil sect, which they referred to as 'The Family'.

Bloody Massacre By Manson And His 'Angels Of Death'

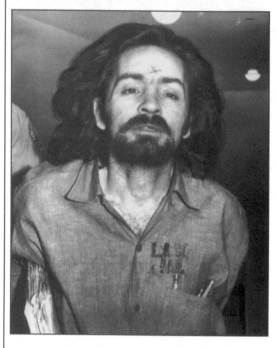

Manson was born in Cincinnati in 1934 to Kathleen Maddox, a 16-year-old prostitute. The name on his birth certificate was No Name Maddox. He never knew who his father was and grew up in an environment of violence and drugs, spending long periods of his adolescence in juvenile institutions. At one detention center, Manson held a blade to a fellow inmate's throat as he violently raped him.

Although mainly homosexual during his teens, Manson married Rosalie Jean Willis, a 17-year-old waitress, in 1954. She was pregnant when he was next sentenced to three years in prison for auto theft. She visited him regularly at the start, bringing Charles Manson Jr. with her, but eventually met someone else and the visits stopped. Manson was never to see his son again. He remarried between jail sentences and had another son, also named Charles Manson Jr., but that marriage also failed.

In 1967 Manson found himself in San Francisco in the heyday of 'flower power' and drug-taking. He had a magnetism that seemed to attract drop-outs and middle-class young women alike. He formed a sect and settled in California's Santa Susana mountains, at Spahn Ranch, a one-time movie set.

Manson was convinced that an uprising between American blacks and whites was coming. He heard messages in the lyrics of Beatles tracks. He prophesied that only his disciples and the 'Chosen Blacks' would survive the mass slaughter and go on to take over the world. His followers, he believed, must rise up and strike out at the white establishment.

He called his devastating plan 'Helter Skelter' and on the night of August 9, 1969, sent four of his disciples—Susan Atkins, Patricia Krenwinkel, Linda Kasabian, and Charles Watson—to 10050 Cielo Drive, Benedict Canyon, Los Angeles, to begin the horrific slaughter. Movie producer, Roman Polanski and his pregnant wife, Sharon Tate, were renting the property. Polanski was

ABOVE: Polish film director Roman Polanski and American actress Sharon Tate at their wedding in 1968.

away filming but Sharon and friends were partying at the house when the self-styled 'Angels of Death' broke in.

They showed no mercy in their frenzied attack. Watson is said to have chanted 'I am the devil come to do the devil's work' as he battered Voytek Frykowski, a Polish movie director, who was then stabbed by Atkins. Jay Sebring a hairdresser, was stabbed and shot.

The most shocking murder was that of heavily pregnant Sharon Tate and her unborn son, who was stabbed 16 times. They tied a nylon rope around her neck, looped it over a ceiling beam and tied the other end around the hooded head of Sebring. Eighteen-year-old Steven Parent, a friend of the Polanskis' caretaker, was shot as he drove from the house. Abigail Folger, a coffee heiress, was slashed to pieces trying to escape the massacre. 'Pigs' was written in blood on the door of the mansion.

There is a theory that Manson's gang had killed the wrong people. The house in Cielo Drive had once been rented by record company boss Terry Melcher, Doris Day's son. He had apparently shunned Manson's attempts at breaking into the recording business.

However, it is also believed that Frykowski and Sebring were drug dealers, whose business Manson coveted.

Displeased with the previous night's messy events at the Tate residence, Manson led the next 'Helter Skelter' mission on August 10. The four Tate murderers were again summoned, along with Steve Grogan and Leslie Van Houten, a former college queen and youngest member of the cult. They cruised the better neighborhoods of Los Angeles in search of potential victims before settling on the home of Leno and Rosemary LaBianca, who owned a small chain of supermarkets. Manson burst into their Waverly Drive mansion, tied them up and left them to the mercy of three of his cult slaves, Watson, Krenwinkel, and Van Houten.

The LaBiancas were subjected to horrific injuries, inflicted with a sword, knives, and forks. 'War' was carved on Leno's stomach and a fork was protruding from his body. He had been stabbed 26 times and, with a blood-soaked pillowcase acting as a hood, symbolically hung. Rosemary also had multiple stab wounds in her back and buttocks, was inscribed with 'War', hooded, and hung. The walls were covered with slogans written in their blood. They had misspelled 'Healter Skelter' on the fridge.

ABOVE: Manson shadowed by police officers in 1970. The spell he managed to cast over his followers was incredible.

The police arrested the Manson 'Family' and, after a sensational trial that lasted 38 weeks, on March 29, 1971, they were all found guilty and sentenced to be executed—commuted to life imprisonment the following year when California quashed the death penalty.

LA5)LOS ANGELES, Dec.2--CULT LEADER?--Charles Manson, above, 34, was described today by the Los Angeles Times and attorney Richard Caballero as the leader of a quasireligious cult of hippies, three of whom have been arrested on murder warrants issued in the slayings of actress Sharon Tate and four others at her home. Manson is in jail

ABOVE: A police mugshot of a crazed-looking Manson after his arrest in 1969.

Los Angeles police did not initially connect the two raids, and it was only the arrest of Susan Atkins in another investigation that brought the evil cult to justice. She was picked up in connection with the slaying of drug dealer Gary Hinman at his Topanga Canyon home 10 days before the mass murders. Atkins could not help boasting about her role in the Tate raid, describing her feelings of sexual satisfaction when stabbing the actress and hearing her scream for mercy. She even claimed she drank Tate's blood.

CALIFORNIA
STATE PRISON
MANSON, C
B-33920
3/18/09

ABOVE: Manson, as he appears today, the swastika tattoo on his forehead a reminder of his sickening past.

Leslie Van Houten succeeded in gaining two retrials in the late 1960s because her lawyer had disappeared during her initial trial. His remains were found later in the mountains, and members of the Manson cult were suspected of his murder. Van Houten failed to win her freedom and was again sentenced to life imprisonment.

America relived the horrific deaths in 1994, when a 'Free Susan Atkins Campaign' was launched. Her supporters felt she was now rehabilitated. However, after hearing evidence from Sharon Tate's sister, Patti, who was only 11 at the time of the murders, her appeal was refused. Patti told of her mother's distress each time a member of the murdering gang applied for parole and of the indifference of the gang as they left behind the sickening murder scene at Cielo Drive and moved on to the massacre at the LaBianca home. Atkins remained in custody, as does Manson, who admits he will kill again if he ever gets his freedom.

ABOVE: Manson during his trial in 1970. He was vowed to kill again if he is ever released from prison.

Peter Manuel

Peter Manuel turned to crime at an early age. When only 11, he was caught breaking into stores. At 15, he attacked a woman with a hammer. As a consequence, he spent a large part of his teen years in an approved school and in Borstal—all of which helped make him a hardened villain ready to turn to violence to obtain either money or sexual satisfaction.

Families Shot Dead By Gun-Toting Burglar

On his release from Borstal in 1946, the 19-year-old Manuel moved to Glasgow, where his Scots-born parents had settled after their Coventry home was destroyed in a German bombing raid. Within weeks, he was arrested for housebreaking and, while awaiting trial, he raped an expectant mother and indecently assaulted two other women. He was sentenced to eight years in jail and was released in 1953.

Three years later, Manuel graduated to murder. His first victim was 17-year-old Annie Knielands, whom he killed in January 1956, and whose body he left on the fifth fairway of a golf course at East Kilbride, near Glasgow. Manuel was questioned and released for lack of evidence. In September 1956, while free on bail over a burglary charge, he broke into a house in Burnside, Glasgow, and shot dead housewife Marion Watt, her sister Margaret, and Marion's 16-year-old daughter Vivienne. Again Manuel was arrested, quizzed and, although he was given 18 months' jail for the earlier burglary, there was insufficient evidence to pin the murders on him.

On his release, Manuel visited Newcastle Upon Tyne for a job interview in early December 1957, where he shot and killed taxi driver Sydney Dunn. Back in

charged with the murder of the Smarts. His father was charged with receiving stolen goods from various burglaries, which, in an attempt to shield his son, he claimed to have bought at a market. Showing remorse for the first time, Manuel offered a full confession in return for his father's release. He led police to the spot where he had thrown two guns into a river and showed them where he had buried Isabelle Cooke.

At his trial, which began in May 1958, Manuel was found guilty of seven murders—although Glasgow police believe he may have killed up to 15 people. The judge commented that 'a man may be very bad without being mad' before sentencing him to death. On July 11, 1958, Peter Manuel was allowed to hear Mass and take Holy Communion before making his final, short walk to the gallows at Glasgow's Barlinnie Jail.

ABOVE: Scottish mass-murderer Peter Manuel smiling during his trial in Glasgow on May 29, 1958.

Glasgow, he struck again on December 27. Isabelle Cooke, aged 17, left her home in Mount Vernon to go to a dance but never returned. Even as police searched for her, three bodies were found in a house just 10 minutes' walk away from Manuel's home. Peter Smart, his wife Doris, and their 11-year-old son Michael had all been shot through the head at close range.

Peter Manuel was arrested on January 14, 1958, and

ABOVE: Manuel is led away by police following his arrest for murder on January 17, 1958.

Robert Maudsley

Robert Maudsley may not be Britain's most prolific serial killer but the jailbird is certainly judged the most dangerous. He committed 'only' four murders—three of them while in prison on a life sentence for the first. His most sickening claim to infamy was taunting jail warders by eating the brains of one of his victims.

Cannibal Killer Ate Prisoner's Brains

Robert John Maudsley was born in Liverpool in 1953, one of 12 children of a violent father. He spent his early years in an orphanage run by nuns. As a teenager, he moved to London and became a rent boy to pay for his drug addiction. In 1974, he attacked a laborer who had picked him up for sex, stabbing him, smashing him over the head with a hammer, and garrotting him. He explained that he had become angry when the man showed him pictures of children he had sexually abused.

Maudsley was given a life sentence and sent to Broadmoor hospital for the criminally insane. There, in February 1977, he and another prisoner, David Cheeseman, dragged convicted pedophile David Francis into a room on their ward, barricaded the door, tied him up with flex from a record player and held him hostage. For 10 hours, staff listened to his screams as he was tortured. Eventually the pair came out, holding the garrotted corpse above their heads as a trophy.

Following this Maudsley was sent to Wakefield Prison, in Yorkshire, where, despite the high security, Prisoner 467637's killing spree continued. In July 1978, Maudsley fashioned a knife from a soup spoon and waited for sex offender Salney Darwood to enter his cell. Maudsley plunged the knife into his back and head, then expertly garrotted him. He stuffed the body under a bunk and went in search of another victim.

Next to die was William Roberts, who was lying face down on his bunk. Maudsley stabbed him then smashed his head against the wall. He is then said to have used his homemade knife to prise open the skull 'like a boiled egg' to scoop out the brains. Afterward, Maudsley strode up to the officer in charge and said: 'There'll be two short on the roll call.'

The incident earned Maudsley the media nickname 'Hannibal the Cannibal', although his fellow inmates referred to him simply as 'Spoons'. Deemed too dangerous for a normal cell, he was placed in solitary confinement in a purpose-built Perspex cage with cardboard furniture and concrete bed beneath Wakefield Prison's F-Wing. Over the next quarter century, he allowed his hair to grow long and his fingernails to 'look more like a vulture's talons', according to one newspaper report.

Maudsley, who enjoys poetry, classical music, and art and has a genius-level IQ, once described life in his 10ft (3m) square cell as 'like being buried alive in a coffin'. He wrote: 'I am left to stagnate; vegetate; and to regress; left to confront my solitary head-on, with people who have eyes but don't see, ears but don't hear, mouths but don't speak; consequently I too am left with no voice, nowhere to turn to but inward.'

Ivan Milat

In September 1992, ramblers in the Belanglo State Forest, New South Wales, Australia, discovered a corpse. The following day, police discovered a second body nearby. The corpses were those of two British girls, 21-year-old Caroline Clarke and 22-year-old Joanne Walters, who had been missing since hitch-hiking from Sydney.

Hitch-Hikers Executed By The 'Backpack Killer'

Caroline had been stabbed and shot in the head several times, the angle of the bullets' entry suggesting to forensic scientists that the killer had used her for target practice. Joanne had been stabbed in the heart and lungs, one cut penetrating her spine and probably paralyzing her before the wounds that finally killed her.

The discoveries sparked a hunt for one of Australia's most notorious and evil serial killers: Ivan Robert Marko Milat. Born in 1945, one of 14 children of a Croat immigrant, he became known as the 'Backpack Killer' because of the way he targeted young hikers. Belanglo State Forest seemed to be his favorite 'killing field'.

Other corpses began turning up in the forest. In October 1993, a walker discovered the remains of James Gibson, and his girlfriend Deborah Everist, both 19 and from Victoria, who had disappeared while hitch-hiking in December 1989. Forensics later confirmed that James had suffered the killer's 'trademark' knife wound through the spine, paralyzing him before he was killed.

The same fate had been suffered by Simone Schmidl, 21, whose body was found the following month. The German girl, missing since January 1991, had been sexually assaulted. Clothing found at the scene was not Schmidl's, however, but matched that of another missing backpacker, 20-year-old Anja Habschied. What was left of Anja and 21-year-old boyfriend Gabor Neuebauer was discovered a few days later. Her head was missing, together with two of her vertebrae. She had been decapitated with a sword while alive and in a kneeling position, Gabor had been gagged and strangled. His skull showed six bullet entries.

It was now clear that a ritualistic serial killer was on the prowl. Police received hundreds of calls from worried parents around the world who wanted assurance that their backpacking children were safe.

ABOVE: The scene outside Campbelltown Local Court in May 1994 as Ivan Milat is charged in relation to the Paul Onions case.

But news of the killing spree also brought the first clue as to the identity of the perpetrator.

British student Paul Onions, 20, had been picked up by a driver in southern New South Wales in January 1990. The man acted so peculiarly that Paul fled and, with his pursuer chasing him gun in hand, Paul flagged down another passing vehicle and escaped. He reported the attack but was told by police that, without the license plate number, there was little chance of tracing the gunman.

Tragically for other, less lucky victims, that proved to be the case. But when Paul Onions repeated his story four years later, police had a description of the 'Backpack Killer'. And when Ivan Milat was subsequently fingered as the prime suspect, Paul was shown a photograph of Milat and was able to identify him straight away.

The final breakthrough came when a woman called to say that her boyfriend worked at a ready-mixed concrete company with a man called Ivan Milat who lived near the forest and was a gun fanatic. Detectives established that Milat had been absent from work on the probable dates of murders, and they pounced on him at his home in Eaglevale while he lay in bed with his girlfriend.

Milat vehemently denied knowledge of the slayings but a search of his house produced items of property belonging to his victims, along with cartridges that matched those found near the backpackers' bodies.

Charged with the seven murders, Milat was finally found guilty on all counts and, in June 1995, was sentenced to life imprisonment. He was taken to a high-security jail in Maitland, southwest of Sydney,

ABOVE: The house of the 'Backpack Killer', Ivan Milat, raided by Australian police in 1994.

bragging that he would one day escape. He made one failed escape attempt in July 1995.

Six years later, a closely-guarded Milat was brought from prison to appear at a reopened inquest into the deaths of three girls who had disappeared in 1978 and 1979 in similar circumstances to those surrounding Milat's other victims. The killer refused to cooperate, and the deaths of the girls, aged 20, 17, and 14, remained unattributed. However, Milat is still suspected of being responsible for many other murders.

Over the years, Milat continued to raise appeals against his conviction. Several times, he injured himself in prison, swallowing razor blades, staples, and other metal objects. In January 2009, he cut off his little finger with a plastic knife, planning to mail it to the High Court.

ABOVE: The prison van used to transport Milat to court to face various charges in May 1994.

Herman Mudgett

Herman Webster Mudgett arrived in Chicago in 1886 with two wives, no money, a fake university degree, and a mission: to get very rich very quickly. He had charm, style, wit, and a way about him that women found irresistible—more often than not, to their cost. Mudgett realized that, in this booming, anything-goes, crime-ridden city preparing to host the World's Fair, he had found the ideal environment in which to carry out his nefarious projects. In so doing, he became America's first identified serial killer.

Secret Gas Chambers In Torturer's Castle

Born in 1860 into a prominent family in Gilmanton, New Hampshire, mustachioed Mudgett was intelligent, handsome, and charming. Kicked out of medical school for stealing cadavers, with which he planned to defraud insurance companies, his knowledge of medicine nevertheless enabled him to pass himself off as a qualified physician, 'Dr Henry Howard Holmes', once he had settled in Chicago.

His first job in that city had been more modest. He took a job as a prescription clerk at a drug store in the Englewood district. After a few months, his employer, a widow, and her young daughter disappeared, Mudgett telling any curious customers that they had moved to California after selling him the store. In fact, Mudgett had killed them.

From his newly acquired base, Mudgett launched a series of dodgy ventures. He bottled tap water as an all-purpose 'miracle cure'. He sold a 'sure-fire cure for alcoholism' at $50 a bottle. And he claimed to have invented a device for turning water into domestic gas that won him a research contract from a utility company. As the money rolled in, he purchased a large plot of land across the road at 701 and 703 Sixty-third Street. It was to be the site of what later became known infamously as Holmes Castle, a three-storey labyrinthine edifice of 100 rooms, with secret passageways, false walls, and mysterious trap-doors.

Mudgett completed his mansion in 1888, when he

LEFT: Herman Mudgett confessed to 27 murders at Holmes Castle, but the true figure may have been as high as 200.

was aged just 28. Over the years, he lured scores of young women to Holmes Castle with the promise of non-existent jobs. There, he would murder his visitors by leaving them in one of the several rooms that were sealed and fed by mysterious pipes. These were his gas chambers. He would then dispose of the bodies in one of two ways—either in his 6ft (2m) wide stove or in barrels of acid.

Mudgett got away with mass murder until September 1894 when he killed a small-time Philadelphia criminal to claim life insurance. A sharp-eyed insurance investigator cast doubt on the claim, and detectives

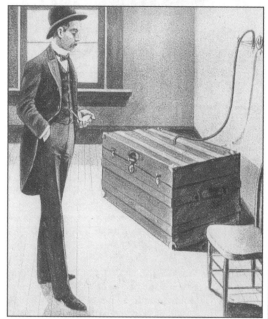

ABOVE: A contemporary print of a detective looking at a trunk fed by a gas pipe—the 'execution chamber' of some of Mudgett's victims.

ABOVE: An ink sketch published at the time of his arrest showing how the 'Torture Castle' killer disposed of his younger victims.

visited the address to where the money was to have been sent: Holmes Castle. What they discovered there is related in a report of the time which describes ordinary bedrooms used for seduction, alongside windowless rooms fed by gas pipes. More horrifically, police believed that in one asbestos-lined chamber he had devised a means of introducing fire, so that the gas pipe became a blow-torch. The basement contained a medieval-style torture rack—and several women's skeletons from which the flesh had been carefully stripped.

Mudgett went on the run but was traced to Boston, where he was arrested in November 1894 planning to flee the country. He was put on trial in Philadelphia for the murder of the petty criminal, although by then it was known that he had also killed the man's three children. After his conviction but while awaiting sentence, he sold his story for $7,500 to Hearst newspapers, in which he confessed to 27 murders in Chicago, Indianapolis, and Toronto.

Although estimates of the number of his victims range up to 200, the true count will never be known. Herman Mudgett was hanged at Philadelphia's Moyamensing Prison on May 7, 1896. He took almost 15 minutes to die.

Dennis Nilsen

Dennis Nilsen was a prolific serial killer, preying on men throughout London in the 1970s and 80s. Insisting he had no control of his actions, he claimed to be in a trance throughout and would 'wake up' to find a dead man in his home. While he argued that his murders were the fault of a personality disorder, the sheer ruthlessness of his killings and disposal of the bodies demonstrated a deadly instinct. Nilsen's own efforts to end his rampage would prove to be his downfall.

Killer Boiled Human Head In A Cookpot

Nilsen killed for the first time in 1978. He picked up a stranger in a pub and they slept together. As dawn broke he realized that he could not bear this newfound bedfellow to leave. He used a tie to strangle the sleeping man, then finished him off by plunging his head into a bucket of water.

Nilsen was at first shocked by his own barbarity but he soon overcame any qualms. His compulsion to kill led to bodies being stored beneath the floorboards of his apartment at Melrose Avenue, Willesden. One nameless victim was so physically appealing to Nilsen that it was a week before the body was put underneath the floor. The killer kept him in the room, returning from work to 'chat' with him and have sex with the corpse.

ABOVE: Dennis Nilsen developed a fascination with corpses, aged five, following the death of his grandfather.

ABOVE: Nilsen at Highgate Magistrates Court, London, during his trial for murder.

simmering on the stove. The body parts, including the boiled head, were put into black plastic bags. Nilsen had no time to dispose of them, however, because neighbors had decided to resolve the plumbing problems by calling in industrial drain clearers.

When an engineer removed a manhole cover, he found decomposing matter was still evident. Police were called and a forensic scientist confirmed that it was human flesh.

When Nilsen returned home from work on February 9, 1983, detectives were waiting for him. He confessed, showing them the bags containing body parts stored in his wardrobe. He went on to relate a macabre series of murderous crimes committed by one of the most unlikely looking villains ever.

For Nilsen just did not look the part of a serial killer. He seemed just too 'ordinary'. Yet it transpired that his

ABOVE: Nilsen's apartment in Melrose Avenue. Victims were murdered and their bodies stored under floorboards.

Another of his many victims had the misfortune to suffer an epileptic fit outside Nilsen's home. Nilsen tended him and, when the man returned the next day to thank him, he was murdered. Nilsen eventually disposed of his stash of corpses by chopping them up and burning them in backyard bonfires.

When Nilsen moved to an apartment at 'Cranley Gardens, Muswell Hill, he no longer had access to a garden, so he was forced to dissect corpses more fully, flushing the skin and bone down the toilet. Eventually the plumbing failed and kindly neighbors posted warning signs on his door. Nilsen knew he had to work fast—for if plumbers entered his apartment, they might find the malodorous body of a 20-year-old man killed the previous week and hidden in his wardrobe.

Nilsen laid plastic sheets across the floor of his front room and, with a kitchen knife, dismembered the body and severed the head, placing it in a large cooking pot fascination with human corpses had been spawned in him when he was very young…

Dennis Andrew Nilsen was born in November 1945 in Fraserburgh, Scotland, the second son of Olav Nilsen, a Norwegian serviceman. Dennis grew up without his father but received enough love and attention from his grandfather, Andrew Whyte, with whom he and his mother lived. When the old man died of a heart attack at the age of 62, he was laid out at home. And it was noted then that little Dennis, just five years old, was fascinated by the corpse. He later admitted that the powerful image of death loomed large in his mind for years.

Aged 16, Nilsen enlisted in the Army, serving as a butcher in the Catering Corps, learning the skills that served him so well during his five-year killing spree. On leaving the Army in 1972, he took up police training

ABOVE: The lack of outside space at Nilsen's apartment in Cranley Gardens led him to flush his victims' remains down the toilet.

ABOVE: Nilsen during his spell in the Army in the 1960s. He worked as a butcher in the Catering Corps.

but resigned and went on to become a recruitment interviewer. In 1975, he moved into the Melrose Road apartment with another man, although the latter denied it was a homosexual relationship. Their friendship lasted two years but when the man left, Nilsen's life began a downward spiral into alcohol and loneliness that culminated in the first murder 18 months later. Nilsen resolved that nobody would walk out on him again— and, for many visitors, that really did mean 'never'.

One visitor who did live to tell the tale was a male model who, during the wave of publicity following Nilsen's arrest in February 1983, told police that he had narrowly escaped death at the hands of the mass killer after meeting Nilsen in a bar and returning with him to his apartment in Cranley Gardens. The model had later awoken gasping for breath, with a swollen tongue and burn marks around his neck. Nilsen had not only tried to strangle him but had also thrust his head into a bucket of water. The would-be victim sought hospital treatment but did not go to the police.

In court, Nilsen's defense counsel tried to persuade the jury that the killer was mad. Thanks in part to the male model's evidence, the panel at the Old Bailey did not believe it. He was found guilty of six murders and two attempted murders. The full tally was reckoned to be at least 15. On November 4, 1983, still showing not a shred of remorse, Dennis Nilsen was jailed for life.

ABOVE: Nilsen during a police interview. He was found guilty of six murders and two attempted murders and jailed for life.

Paul Ogorzow

In 1940, as German tanks rolled across Europe, a few more acts of savagery would hardly be an issue for the Nazi hierarchy—or so one would have thought. But a few seemingly isolated events in the German capital gave more concern to the authorities than their actual numbers might have otherwise warranted.

Hushed-Up Shame Of Nazi Era Cops

Over the summer months, three women had been stabbed and two others assaulted in the eastern districts of Berlin. Now, as winter approached, women's bodies began turning up. In October, a 20-year-old mother of two was stabbed in the neck and strangled. A month later, a 30-year-old was thrown unconscious from a moving train but survived. In December, a 26-year-old nurse was beaten to death and thrown from a train. On the same day, and only 550 yards (500m) away, a 19-year-old girl had her skull smashed and was raped.

Just before Christmas, a 30-year-old woman was found with a fractured skull. The next victim, a 46-year-old with similar injuries, was found a week later. Another body, of a woman aged 28, turned up in January 1941. Police believed all or most of the victims

had been attacked on a train or near a rail track.

The attacker, now labeled 'the S-Bahn (City Railroad) Murderer', brought terror to the capital. While the world recoiled at the mounting death toll of World War Two, Berliners concentrated on the slaughter of innocents closer to home. Not that they had much information to go on...

The Nazi propaganda machine, under Joseph Goebbels, wanted only 'good' news, so the murders were only publicized in brief detail for fear of causing public panic. Other factors hampered Berlin's serious crime force, the Kriminalpolizei, in their hunt for the serial killer. A blackout was being enforced in the city and this had proved a dream for criminals and a nightmare for the police. The blackout also caused numerous travel accidents, with an average of one fatality every day on the railroad system. It was initially difficult to distinguish between an accident and a homicide.

The result of these drawbacks was that there were two more victims. The body of a 39-year-old woman was found in February beside the railroad line, evidently having been thrown from a train, and in early

July, the body of a woman of 35 was discovered with similar injuries on waste ground.

Despite the problems caused by wartime restrictions, the Kriminalpolizei had been tardy in identifying the killer. All evidence had pointed to a railroad employee, yet it took several preventable deaths before detectives finally arrested an S-Bahn signalman, Paul Ogorzow, 28, who lived with his wife and two children close to where four of his victims were found.

Shamefully, the police realized that they had already questioned their suspect after a tip-off but had let him go, and on another occasion when challenged by Kriminalpolizei officers, he had simply fled into the night. The tip-off had come from the killer's railroad colleagues, who had long suspected him because of his loudly voiced hatred of women and his habit of vanishing for long spells while on duty.

Ogorzow was charged with eight murders, six cases of attempted murder, and a further 31 cases of assault. In court, he declared himself a family man, loyal Nazi Party member, and an active street fighter with the SA. But the judge agreed he was 'a killer of a completely cold and calculating nature, with depraved sexual urges'. He was executed by guillotine in Plötzensee Prison.

Anatoly Onoprienko

When police seized Anatoly Onoprienko, otherwise known as 'The Terminator', they locked up the worst serial killer the Ukraine had ever known. Onoprienko, a 37-year-old former forestry student, sailor, and mental hospital outpatient, was arrested in April 1996 at his girlfriend's apartment, where police found a shotgun matching the one used in no fewer than 40 murders. The total number of his victims was 52.

Bloody Trail Of 'The Terminator'

Onoprienko eventually confessed to all 52 murders in a six-year killing spree, in which he claimed he was commanded by 'inner voices'. Onoprienko's rampage began in June 1989, when he and accomplice Serhiy Rogozin robbed and killed nine people. They first blasted a couple to death in their car, then wiped out of a family of five, including an 11-year-old girl.

Onoprienko spent six years traveling around Eastern Europe, where police believe he may have been responsible for other murders. Onoprienko resumed the known killings in late 1995, and they followed a set pattern. He would choose an isolated house, storm in at dawn, round up the family and shoot them all, including the children, at close range with a 12-gauge shotgun. Any witnesses would also be dispatched.

ABOVE: Anatoly Onoprienko, aka The Terminator, is Ukraine's worst ever serial killer, with a body count of 52.

He would hack off fingers to get at wedding rings and even pull out his victims' gold teeth. He would then loot the house before setting it on fire.

In November 1995, after stealing a shotgun, he began a killing spree that at one stage went into manic overdrive—in just one 20-week bloodbath, he killed and mutilated 43 people in the Lvov region, near the border of Poland. Victims ranged from a 70-year-old pensioner to a three-month-old baby. Panic was so widespread in two villages, Bratkovichi and Busk, that the army was sent in, personnel carriers patrolled the streets and police imposed a security cordon.

A manhunt involving 2,000 police and more than 3,000 troops failed to find 'The Terminator'. In the end, a tip-off about an unlicensed gun led detectives, on April 14, 1996, to an apartment in the garrison town of Yavoriv. Onoprienko was sleeping beside his girlfriend—to whom he had once proposed with a ring he had chopped from the finger of one of his victims only a few hours earlier. Ordered out of bed, Onoprienko furtively withdrew a gun from a cupboard, but handcuffs were clapped on him before he could pull the trigger.

In February 1999, a court in the city of Zhytomyr, 90 miles (140km) west of Kiev, ruled that Onoprienko was mentally competent to answer charges. The 39-year-old killer sat impassively in a metal cage as a woman screamed from the back of the court: 'Let us tear him apart. He should die a slow and agonizing death.' The judge commented: 'He doesn't care about anything—

ABOVE: During a prison interview, Onoprienko claimed: 'I have never felt sorry for those I killed. No love, no hatred, just blind indifference.'

only about himself. He is driven by extreme cruelty.' Onoprienko was sentenced to death, later commuted to life in prison.

Explaining his murderous drive, Onoprienko said in a prison interview: 'To me killing people is like ripping up a duvet. Women, old people, children, they are all the same. I have never felt sorry for those I killed. No love, no hatred, just blind indifference.'

William Palmer

Deep in debt and gambling wildly, Dr William Palmer cheered up somewhat when the friend he was accompanying to the races won more than £2,000—a small fortune in 1855. Palmer, aged 31, watched as the lucky winner, 28-year-old John Parsons Cooke, drained a celebratory brandy and gasped: 'Good God, there's something in it—it burns my throat.' Palmer himself nonchalantly knocked back the few remaining drops in the bottom of the glass. In front of a witness he declared: 'Nonsense, there is nothing in it.'

How Dr Palmer The Poisoner Gambled And Lost

In pain, Cooke left the racecourse at Shrewsbury, Shropshire, and traveled the 40 miles (64km) to the doctor's home town of Rugeley, Staffordshire, where he stayed at an inn, which Palmer's visited regularly to treat his patient. Strangely, the medicine and broths prescribed only seemed to make Cooke worse.

ABOVE: Dr William Palmer on the stand during his trial at the Central Criminal Court in London, in May 1856.

ABOVE: The high street in Rugeley, Staffordshire, where Palmer murdered his 'friend' John Parsons Cooke.

Only when the bookmakers had paid out Cooke's winnings, swiftly pocketed by Palmer, did the doctor finish him off. After suffering convulsions for several days, Cooke went rigid in spasms and finally suffocated—the symptoms of strychnine poisoning.

Cooke, it transpired, was far from being Palmer's first victim in a medical career that was disgracefully blighted. By the time he was 17, he had already been dismissed from two pharmacy apprenticeships, once for taking cash and the second time for running an illegal abortion service. He finally qualified as a doctor in London in 1846 and the following year married Anne

LEFT: A period sketch of Dr Palmer at the horse races. He was known as the 'Prince of Poisoners'.

Brookes, the heiress daughter of a wealthy widow.

Palmer paid little heed to his family or to his doctor's practice, instead spending his days at racecourses. As his debts mounted, however, a string of deaths occurred in his family. First, Palmer's rich mother-in-law died, followed by his wife, who had been heavily insured. Palmer's brother, four children, an uncle, and several more of his creditors met similar ends.

Palmer became both greedy and impatient. And it was his blatant poisoning of his friend Cooke in 1855 that ended his one-man crime wave. Arrested and brought to trial at London's Old Bailey, he heard medical evidence that only strychnine poisoning could have produced such symptoms—and that the day before his friend's death, the doctor had bought a bottle of strychnine from a local chemist.

The jury was out for only 100 minutes before returning a guilty verdict and Palmer was sentenced to be hanged at Stafford Prison. Interviewed there by the governor, the condemned man replied: 'I have nothing more to say than this—that I am quite easy in my conscience and happy in my mind.' To the very end, he refused to confess. He insisted he had been unjustly convicted of murder by strychnine—though lawyers believed this was his way of hinting that he had killed his friend by some other means. Indeed, his last remark made to the priest who visited him before his execution was: 'Cooke did not die from strychninia.'

Such was the sensational nature of the case that an estimated 25,000 people flocked to Stafford by road, rail, on horseback, and on foot to cheer the evil doctor's hanging at eight o'clock on the morning of June 14, 1856.

Carl Panzram

Carl Panzram wrote from his cell on Death Row in Leavenworth Prison, Kansas, in 1929: 'In my lifetime, I have murdered 21 human beings. I have committed thousands of burglaries, robberies, larcenies, arsons and, last but not least, I have committed sodomy on more than 100 male human beings. For all these things I am not in the least bit sorry.'

'I Hate The Whole Damned Human Race'

Born of Prussian immigrant parents in Warren, Minnesota, in 1891, Panzram had been in trouble with police from the age of eight, when he was arrested for being drunk and disorderly! Three years later, a string of burglaries landed him in reform school—which he tried to burn down, with some success. Freed at the age of 13, he had already gained the knowledge he needed for his life of crime: 'how to steal, lie, hate, burn and kill,' as he later wrote in his autobiography.

Panzram joined the US Army at 16 but was so rebellious that he was court-martialed and jailed for three years—the first of several terms in prison. He went on to murder indiscriminately all over the world, but his principal areas of operation were West Africa, Mexico, California, Montana, and Washington DC.

His two most infamous crimes were committed in the 1920s. Panzram bought a yacht, the *John O'Leary* (which was also one of his aliases) and lured 10 crewmen aboard with the promise of unlimited bootleg liquor. The men were given alcohol until they were senseless, then were raped and murdered, their bodies thrown overboard. Later, in Portuguese West Africa, he hired 10 locals to accompany him on a crocodile hunt. He killed them all, sodomizing their corpses before feeding them to the crocs.

In 1928 he was jailed at Leavenworth for 20 years for another murder. He told the warden: 'I'll kill the first man who crosses me'—and carried out his threat by battering to death a civilian employee with an iron bar. He was sentenced to death, spurning attempts at a reprieve by telling liberal campaigners: 'I believe the only way to reform people is to kill them.'

He went to the gallows on September 5, 1930, berating his executioner: 'Hurry up, you bastard, I could hang a dozen men while you're fooling around.' The remorseless killer left behind an autobiography in which he summed up his philosophy in three defiant sentences: 'I don't believe in Man, God nor Devil'; 'I hate the whole damned human race, including myself', and 'I wish the whole world had but a single throat and I had my hands around it.'

Elaine Parent

Elaine Antoinette Parent traveled the world under at least 20 stolen identities and eluded investigators for 12 years. Although hunted by police for killing and mutilating one female victim, she is feared to have murdered and stolen the identities of many more.

The 'Chameleon' Who Stole Other People's Lives

New York-born Parent, nicknamed 'The Chameleon', was an expert con-artist; bisexual, beautiful, clever, and deadly. This is how she operated…

In early 1990, lonely bank employee Beverly McGowan, 34, placed a newspaper advertisement for someone to share her Miami condominium. A woman in her late 40s, calling herself 'Alice', answered the advert, and swiftly moved in. Beverly told her brother, Steve, about her charming new roommate and said she felt her life 'had turned around'. Indeed, it was about to.

Pretending to be an expert on numerology, and promising to predict a rosy future for her, the newcomer convinced Beverly to part with her date and time of birth and her credit card and driver's license numbers.

On July 8, someone using the name Beverly McGowan called her place of work to take a day off sick. A day later, brother Steve received a goodbye letter supposedly from Beverly, saying that she was leaving home for a while. Knowing this to be uncharacteristic behavior, he called at his sister's condo and, finding her missing, stopped her credit cards.

At about the same time that Steve arrived at her front door, however, a mutilated and decapitated corpse was being recovered from a remote canal bank in southern Florida. The female's head and hands had been hacked off at the wrists with a chainsaw to delay identification, a hole in her stomach had been gouged out to eradicate the identifying tattoo that lay there, and only five teeth and half a jaw remained. But the killer had missed the tattoo of a rose on the woman's ankle and police were able to identify the body as Beverly McGowan's.

A few days later, 'Alice' tried to use Beverly's canceled credit card to book a flight to London and rent a car. Nobody by the name of Alice or Beverly McGowan turned up at Heathrow Airport, and when the credit card transactions failed, the investigation became an international manhunt. 'Alice', however, disappeared.

Six years later, after reinvestigating the manifest for the 1990 flight to London, detectives concentrated on a passenger listed as 'Sylvia Ann Hodgkinson'. They found that Hodgkinson was a deceased British citizen and had three other identities linked to her: Charlotte Rae Cowan, Ann Tremont, and Elaine Antoinette Parent.

Inquiries back in Florida revealed that Parent, using the alias Ann Tremont, had befriended a woman in a bar in Orlando in 1989 and, using numerology to obtain vital information, had stolen her identity. A modus operandi was emerging that made Elaine Parent prime suspect for the murder of Beverly McGowan.

Forensic investigators now re-examined the writing pad supposedly used by Beverly in her 'goodbye' letter. Impressions on the pad revealed hidden correspondence in Parent's handwriting—the content being angry threats to an ex-lover living in London, where Parent had fled in 1990. The lover, a businesswoman, told police of Parent's violent mood swings. Another ex-lover revealed that she was sometimes so frightened of Parent that she would drive 80 miles (128km) to a friend's house to escape.

In April 2002, Parent, then aged 60, was finally tracked down to a house in Panama City, Florida, where she was using the name 'Darlene Thompson'. When police called to arrest her, she asked if she could change her clothes. She went back into the bedroom—and fired a shot through her heart with a .375 Magnum.

To this day, police still don't know how many identities Elaine Parent acquired, and they fear several more women suffered the same fate as Beverly McGowan. The full extent of secretive Parent's homicidal history may never be known.

Leszek Pekalski

When Leszek Pekalski confessed to 70 murders, he became infamous as Poland's most prolific serial killer. Whether he really did slaughter so many is unlikely, and the true figure may never be known, for Pekalski later retracted his confession. But police believe that a tally of 17 butchered and abused female victims is a sad certainty.

'I'm Just A Weak Man' Claims Killer

Born in 1966 at Osieki near Bytów, Poland, Pekalski was deserted by his father and abused by his mother before she also abandoned him. Raised by nuns, he was never able to form a normal relationship and instead discovered that by attacking women, he could control them—beating, stabbing or strangling his victims in order to have sex with them.

Pekalski first killed when, at the age of only 16, he pounced on a 13-year-old girl playing in the countryside on a school outing. It launched him on a reign of terror lasting a dozen years as the misfit became a wanderer, traveling the length and breadth of his homeland.

A detective later said: 'We couldn't find his trail. He never followed a regular pattern. There was no typical victim or a repeated killing method. He would hit with a wooden cane or would strangle his victim with a belt.'

Yet a chance to stop Pekalski was lost in 1990 when he was arrested on suspicion of rape and positively identified by the victim. The investigating officers merely ordered that he attend a psychiatric examination. He was finally given a two-year suspended sentence—and the killing spree continued.

Now labeled the 'Vampire of Bytów', he went on to beat a 17-year-old girl to death with a metal post in woods near her home. The sick killer watched from a hideout as the girl's devastated father discovered the body. Pekalski spoke too openly about the killing, however, and in 1992 police interviewed him as a suspect. He made a handwritten confession, claiming he had committed 70 murders, but, by the time he appeared in court in the northern city of Slupsk, he had changed his mind.

He told the magistrate: 'I'm a gullible man and I was easily persuaded by what the officers had told me. I'm mentally weak and if somebody pushes me I break down. Then I admit to things I have never done. I have never killed anyone. I'm so scared.'

The accused man struck a pitiful pose in the dock and, to the anger of the dead women's families, the magistrate said he could not 'help feeling vaguely sorry for him'. The case faltered when DNA evidence was ruled to be 'contaminated'. However, police witnesses insisted that Pekalski's confession included details of crimes that no one but the killer could have known.

The trial dragged on for eight months. Victims' families were furious when, in 1994, the 17 murder charges against him resulted in only one conviction for a single killing. He was cleared of the others on the grounds of insufficient evidence. Pekalski was sentenced to 25 years in a psychiatric institute, where an initial report judged him, not unexpectedly, to have 'an abnormal sex drive'.

Marcel Petiot

When Dr Marcel Andre Felix Petiot became mayor of Villeneuve-sur-Yonne, in Burgundy, he seemed a paragon of respectability. Yet strange events began to occur in the French town. In 1928 the mayor's pregnant housekeeper vanished without trace. Two years later a woman patient was murdered. A friend who pointed the finger of blame at the doctor also mysteriously fell ill and died. Petiot signed the death certificate.

Treacherous Doctor Death Dies By The Guillotine

How Petiot ever got to become mayor in the first place is as astonishing as his becoming a doctor. Born in Auxerre, 100 miles (160km) south of Paris, in 1897, the young Marcel was expelled from school for circulating obscene photographs to other children. He also enjoyed torturing animals to death.

An early career of petty crime was foreshortened when, in January 1916, with World War One in progress, he was drafted into the French infantry. He was discharged in 1917 with the recommendation that he enter an asylum. Instead, he took advantage of an education program for war veterans, trained as a doctor and, amazingly, qualified.

Petiot began a practice in the town of Villeneuve-sur-Yonne, where he married, had a son and eventually became mayor. He stole from the townspeople,

ABOVE: Marcel Petiot speaks from the dock during his trial at the Palais de Justice in March 1946.

ABOVE: Petiot in the dock, with his lawyer Dr Fleuriot, in the foreground.

overcharged his patients, and cheated on his wife, having an affair with a young woman whose dismembered body was found in a river. When his housekeeper died in mysterious circumstances, Petiot was accused of her murder. The charges had to be dropped, however, when the case files disappeared.

Petiot and his family moved in 1933 to Paris, where he set himself up in a practice on the Rue Caumartin. He thrived by supplying drugs to addicts and carrying out illegal abortions until, charged with stealing from a dead patient, he pleaded insanity and was sent to a mental hospital.

Released in time for the outbreak of World War Two,

RIGHT: Charged with multiple counts of murder, crazed Petiot claimed he was in fact a hero of the French Reistance.

Petiot pretended to be a member of the French Resistance and offered to aid refugees, mainly Jewish, who were trapped in Paris when the Nazis took the city in 1940. Instead, he robbed and murdered them.

The bodies of dozens of these unfortunates were found in his cellar when firemen were called to his elegant house at Rue Lesueur, in the fashionable Etoile district, in March 1944. Neighbors had complained of thick, black, foul smelling smoke spewing from the chimney. Firemen soon discovered the cause—the flames of a coal burning furnace consuming human arms, legs, and torsos in every state of dismemberment. In an outhouse were several corpses covered with lime. Petiot fled and really did join the Resistance, using the name 'Henri Valery'. Finally arrested in October 1944, he put up an outraged defense, passing himself off as a hero of *La Liberation*. At his trial at the Palais de Justice in March 1946, the jury were initially sympathetic—until they heard how the doctor had injected an entire Jewish family 'for typhoid' then watched through a peephole as they died in agony.

Petiot admitted killing 19 of the 27 victims found at Rue Lesueur but denied any knowledge of a further 44 identified victims. Sentenced to death by guillotine, he cried out to his wife Georgette: 'You must avenge me.' Her appeals for presidential clemency failed, however, and the evil doctor's head was laid on the block of the guillotine early in the morning of May 25, 1946.

ABOVE: The jury at Petiot's trial learned how the evil doctor had administered lethal injections to an entire Jewish family.

Waltraud Wagner and colleagues

A doctor was having a quiet after-work drink in a Vienna bar in February 1989 when he overheard parts of a conversation from an adjoining table. The bar was close to the city's Lainz General Hospital, and the table was occupied by a group of nursing aides who were employed there. The women were giggling over the death of an elderly patient—who had been treated to something they called the 'water cure' for refusing medication and calling one of the nurses, Waltraud Wagner, 'a common slut'.

'Water Cure' By The Angels Of Death

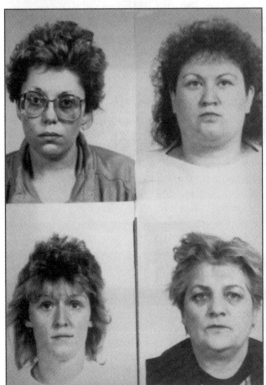

ABOVE: The 'Angels of Death', clockwise from top left: Waltraud Wagner, Maria Gruber, Stefanie Mayer, and Irene Leidolf.

The doctor seated nearby could pick up only snatches of the conversation but they were enough to shock him. He went to the police, who launched a six-week investigation that led to the arrest of Wagner and three other nurses. Together, they comprised one of the most unusual crime teams in 20th century Europe, and were subsequently proven to have murdered scores of patients in their care.

The ringleader, Wagner, had been 23 when she claimed her first victim in 1983. Disposing of a patient with an overdose of morphine, she discovered the thrill of wielding the power of life and death over her elderly charges. She recruited Maria Gruber, 19, Irene Leidolf, 21, and the senior member of the group, 43-year-old Stephanija Mayer.

For the next six years, the evil foursome gave death a helping hand at Lainz hospital, which specialized in geriatric cases. Officially, the body count would stand at 42, but many put the final tally at between 200 and 300 victims.

Since lethal injections failed to provide sufficient excitement, the 'Angels of Death' devised their own murder method. Usually working on the night shift, one would hold the victim's head and nose, while another would pour water into the victim's mouth, causing drowning. Since elderly patients were frequently found to have fluid in their lungs, it seemed an unprovable crime.

When arrested after their loose-tongued drinking session in 1989, Wagner was first to crack, confessing to 39 killings. She said: 'The ones who got on my nerves were dispatched to a free bed with the good Lord. They sometimes resisted but we were stronger. We could decide whether the old fools lived or died. Their ticket to God was long overdue anyway.'

ABOVE: Defendant Irene Leidolf testifies during her trial on March 4, 1991. She was convicted of five murders.

Although she later reduced her confession to only 10 cases of 'mercy killing', a court in March 1991 sentenced her to life for 15 murders and 17 attempted murders. Irene Leidolf also got a life sentence for five murders, Stephanija Mayer 15 years for manslaughter and seven attempted murders, and Maria Gruber 15 years for two attempted murders.

Austrian Chancellor Franz Vranitzky labeled the Lainz murder spree 'the most brutal and gruesome crime in our nation's history'.

Frederick and Rose West

In October 1996, Gloucester City Council demolished 25 Cromwell Street, crushing every brick so that no souvenirs could be taken of Britain's most infamous 'House of Horrors'. The house had been the site of such unspeakable depravity, cruelty, and torture that there could be no other course of action. Two years earlier, the mutilated bodies of nine of the victims of Frederick and Rosemary West had been discovered buried in the cellar or under the patio, ending a killing spree which had lasted for more than two decades, and resulted in Fred being charged with 12 murders, and Rose convicted of 10.

'House Of Horrors' Couple Killed Their Own Kids

Frederick and Rosemary met in 1969 when Rosemary was just 15 years old and already dabbling in prostitution. She was living with her mother Daisy and two younger brothers. They had escaped her violent and incestuous father, although Rosemary moved back in with him after becoming intimate with West and it is said that she still had sex with her father, with West's consent, even after their marriage.

In this respect, Frederick's childhood was very similar to Rose's. He was his mother's favorite of three sisters and two younger brothers and it is rumored that he was just 12 when she seduced him. His father treated his children as sexual playthings and Frederick grew up believing it natural to behave in this way. Indeed, when questioned by police in 1961 accused of child abuse by impregnating a 13-year-old, he commented: 'Doesn't everyone do it?'

By the time West became acquainted with Rose, he had already murdered at least once if not more. He was married at the time to Rena Costello, reputedly a prostitute, who already had a baby daughter, Charmaine. The couple soon had a child of their own, Anne-Marie, and a friend of Rena's, Ann McFall, moved in to help with childcare.

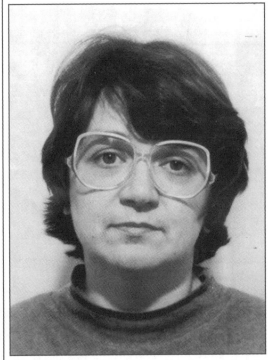

ABOVE: Evil Fred West grew up thinking that incest and rape was normal behavior. He committed suicide while awaiting trial in 1995.

ABOVE: Rosemary West was convicted on 10 counts of murder, including those of her own children.

Ann became infatuated with Frederick, willingly taking part in his sadistic sex games, so Rena moved out, leaving the girls with their father. Ann, now heavily pregnant with West's baby, constantly urged West to divorce Rena but, unwilling to do so, he murdered Ann instead, removing her fingers and toes—later to become his signature mutilation—and burying her in a field in Kempley, Gloucestershire, along with the body of her unborn baby.

On moving in with West in 1969, Rose took the role of surrogate mother to Charmaine and Anne-Marie, and in October 1970 gave birth to her own daughter,

ABOVE: Fred and Rose look the epitome of a normal loving couple in this photograph...yet they were anything but.

Heather, thought to be her father's incestuous child. Poor little Charmaine had a pitiful existence, abused by the couple and subjected to regular beatings. It is believed that Rose murdered Charmaine during a savage attack while Fred was serving a short prison sentence for burglary in 1971, hiding her body until his release, when he removed her toes and fingers and buried her at 25 Midland Road, Gloucester, their home at the time. When Rena came to visit her daughter, West also murdered her and buried her in the field in Kempley.

Fred and Rose married in 1972 and had their second daughter, Mae, in June that year. They moved into the much larger 25 Cromwell Street, enabling them to take in boarders to help with the bills. Fred fitted the cellar

ABOVE: Heather West was murdered by her parents in June 1987 and her body buried under the patio.

out as a torture chamber to enable him to engage in his sexual fantasies involving young girls, and Rose, still operating as a part-time prostitute, had a red light outside her bedroom so that the children knew not to enter when mummy was busy. Eight-year-old Anne-Marie became a regular victim of their sadistic games, held down by Rose while Fred violently raped her and threatened with more violence if she told anyone.

Rose was often pregnant, and gave birth to Tara in 1977, Louise in 1978, Barry in 1980, Rosemary Junior in 1982, and Lucyanna in 1983. Tara, Rosemary, and

ABOVE: West buried the body of his first known victim, Ann McFall, in a field in Gloucestershire...minus her finger and toes.

ABOVE: Fred West turned the cellar at his 25 Cromwell Street home into a torture chamber.

Lucyanna were not Fred's children. During this period, as the family expanded, so too did the Wests' insatiable perversions.

In the space of five years, the couple's appetites for violence and sex games resulted in the brutal murders of eight young women, lured by the couple into their home either as boarders or picked-up hitch-hiking or at bus-stops and taken home to be used as sexual playthings. They all suffered horrendous torture and rape. Sometimes West would wrap their heads tightly in brown tape and insert breathing tubes into their nostrils while he subjected them to his sexual deviations involving whips and chains, rape, and bestiality. Once dead, they would be mutilated and buried under floorboards, in the cellar or under the patio.

One willing participant to their games was 18-year-old Shirley Robinson, who engaged in three-in-a-bed sex sessions with the couple. However, she fell in love with Fred and became pregnant with his child. Rose became jealous, despite the fact that she was pregnant at the time by a West Indian visitor. She put pressure on Fred, and Shirley vanished in May 1978. Her body was discovered in the garden on 25 Cromwell Street, along with that of her unborn child.

Their next victim was 16-year-old Alison Chambers, who moved in to become their nanny. She was last seen in August 1979 and was found underneath the lawn.

Fred's sexual interest in his own daughters did not wane and, after Anne-Marie moved out to live with a boyfriend, he switched his attentions to Heather and Mae. Despite violence and threats, Heather managed to resist his incestuous acts, confiding in a friend. She disappeared in June 1987. Her parents pretended she had run away. In fact, she was buried under the patio— a fate promised to the Wests' other children and joked about by them when later interviewed by police.

The Wests were arrested in 1992 following allegations of child abuse, and their five children under 16 were taken into care. The police found evidence of child abuse, including rape and buggery, but the case against them collapsed when two key witnesses refused to testify. However, Detective-Constable Hazel Savage of Gloucestershire Police was convinced something terrible was going on at 25 Cromwell Street. Investigating further and coaxing information from the West children, she persisted, despite the skepticism of senior officers, and obtained a search warrant in February 1994. The following day, the digging began— and Fred and Rosemary were arrested.

Fred escaped trial for the 12 murders, as he hung himself in his cell on New Year's Day 1995. Rosemary was brought to trial in October 1995 and found guilty of 10 murders, including those of her own children. She was sentenced to life, with the judge's recommendation that she should never be released.

Police believe that they may have murdered many more young girls, as there was an eight-year gap between the murder of Alison Chambers in 1979 and that of Heather in 1987. Without their bodies, the true number of their victims will never be known.

Wayne Williams

When Wayne Bertram Williams was arrested in 1981 as chief suspect in the 'Atlanta Child Murders', the killings that had caused two years of terror throughout the Georgia capital suddenly ended. And after his conviction the following year, Atlanta police declared 25 of the 30 murders solved.

Riddle Of Pudgy Geek And The 30 Child Murders

On February 27, 1982, Wayne Williams was led to the cells, tear-stained and still protesting his innocence, to serve a double sentence of life imprisonment. However, it did not end the debate over whether Williams should have borne the blame for the entire string of Georgian slayings.

Many black citizens, including some families of the victims, believed the state had manufactured much of the evidence to bring the case to a close. For although the crimes were labeled 'child murders', Williams was convicted of only two of the 30 homicides investigated—and those two murders were of adults.

The series of killings loosely (perhaps too loosely) tagged the 'Atlanta Child Murders' began in July 1979 were baying for justice. But months after the slaughter of the innocents started, Atlanta Police could find no pattern beyond the fact that the victims were mainly young black males. They had been stabbed, shot or strangled and their bodies were found dumped throughout the city in creeks, woods vacant lots, under floors, and in the Chattahoochee River.

On the night of May 22, 1981 teams of officers were monitoring cars using main routes around Atlanta. A police recruit on the Jackson Parkway bridge over the Chattahoochee heard a splash—and shortly afterward Williams's car was stopped as it crossed the bridge. Along with many other drivers, he was questioned, his name taken and was allowed to go.

Two days after that face-to-face encounter with a killer, the body of a 27-year-old petty thief was fished out of the river, followed two days later by the body of a 21-year-old. Both had been strangled. Police reviewed the names taken on the bridge earlier and came up with that of Wayne Bertram Williams.

ABOVE: Wayne Williams was convicted of double homicide, but it is believed he was responsible for 24 other murders.

ABOVE: The prosecution in Williams's trial matched 19 different sources of fibers from around his home to a number of the victims.

when the bodies of two black children, 13-year-old Alfred Evans and 14-year-old Edward Smith, were found in undergrowth. They had been strangled. Further young victims were discovered in September and November. The first female victim, a 12-year-old, was found tied to a tree with someone else's panties forced down her throat. She had been sexually abused before being strangled.

Within a year of the first attacks, victims were turning up at the rate of one per month. The dead were aged between seven and 14, and all but two were boys. When the number of unsolved deaths reached 26, the public

ABOVE: Williams vehemently protested his innocence after his arrest in May 1981.

A surveillance team put a watch on the podgy 23-year-old, who lived with his parents, both teachers, in the Atlanta suburb of Dixie Hills, from where many of the victims came. A solitary figure, he was known as a 'scanner freak' because he spent hours tuned into short-wave radio to monitor police and ambulance activity. When an incident occurred, he would rush to the scene, photograph the action and try to sell the images to local newspapers and television stations.

Williams was arrested, still vehemently protesting his innocence. During his two-month trial, which began in January 1982, the prosecution matched 19 different sources of fibers from around his home to a number of the victims. Most significantly, dog hairs taken from the clothes of the thief found in the river on May 24 matched those in Williams's car. There was also eyewitness testimony placing Williams with different victims.

Williams was only ever charged with the murders of the two adults fished out of the Chattahoochee. But a crucial ruling by the judge allowed the prosecution to introduce evidence which linked him with other victims even though he was not accused of their murders. The prosecution, whose case had previously hung literally by a hair, were now able to paint Williams as a predatory homosexual, who they argued was guilty of all the murders.

On February 27, the jury deliberated for 10 hours before finding him guilty and he was sentenced to two consecutive terms of life imprisonment. Appeals for a retrial have consistently been rejected.

Steve Wright

The winter of 2006 saw Britain's biggest manhunt since the search for the Yorkshire Ripper (see page 197). It began with the discovery of the bodies of five murdered women in scattered locations near Ipswich, in Suffolk. All had been working as prostitutes in the town's red light district. Police immediately warned women off the streets and appealed for clues to the killer. More than 500 officers were drafted in to work on the case, and the number of calls received to the public information line reached 10,000.

The Killer Hooked On Hookers

The murders took place during November and December 2006. The bodies of the five women, aged between 19 and 29, were discovered naked but with no signs of sexual assault. Two of the victims had been asphyxiated but cause of death for the other three was not established. In a macabre twist, two of the women's bodies had been carefully arranged in a crucifix shape.

On December 19, police arrested a local man, Steve Wright, who lived within the red light district itself and whom they knew as a habitual user of prostitutes. Wright, born in the Norfolk village of Erpingham in 1958, had joined the merchant navy after leaving school, and followed that with jobs as a docker, a steward on the liner *QE2*, a lorry driver, a barman, and finally a fork-lift truck driver. He had two children, one from a nine-year marriage that ended in 1987, another out of wedlock in 1992. Wright was an inveterate gambler with large debts and had recently been declared bankrupt. He had twice tried to commit

RIGHT: Fork-lift truck driver, Steve Wright, was a known user of prostitutes and lived in Ipswich's red light district.

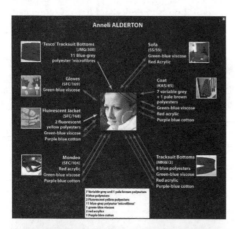
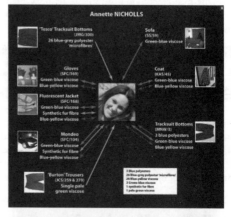
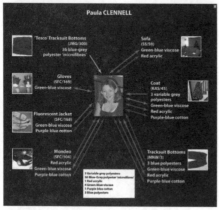
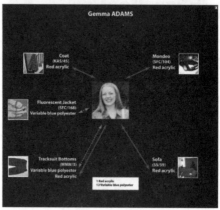

ABOVE: Top row left: Anneli Alderton, 24, was in the early stages of pregnancy when she disappeared on December 3. Top row right: The forensic evidence linking Wright to the murder of Annette Nichols—including tracksuit bottoms, gloves, fluorescent jacket, and samples found in his Ford Mondeo car. Bottom row left: Paula Clennell disappeared shortly after midnight on December 10. She worked as a prostitute to fund her drug addiction. Bottom row right: The body of 25-year-old Gemma Adams was found on December 2, in a river at Hintlesham.

suicide, the last attempt in 2000 with an overdose of pills. At his trial, which began at Ipswich Crown Court in December 2007, Wright admitted hiring the girls for sex but denied any connection with their deaths. The prosecution produced DNA and fiber evidence that linked him to the victims. In a surprise move, it was also suggested that Wright may not have acted alone, as the remains of one girl was found some distance from the road but with no sign of her body being dragged there by a single person.

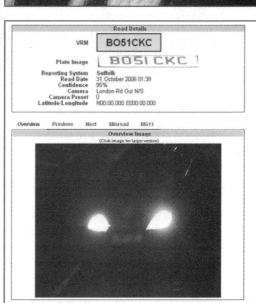

ABOVE: The jury in Steve Wright's trial visit Coddock Mill, Suffolk, where Tania Nicol's body was found.

ABOVE RIGHT: An artist's impression of Steve Wright, appearing at Ipswich Crown Court on January 14, 2008.

RIGHT: Wright's car license plate captured on camera on a road near where one of the bodies was discovered.

In February 2008, Wright was found guilty of all five murders and was jailed for life, with the recommendation that he should never be considered for parole. Mr Justice Gross told him: 'Drugs and prostitution meant (the girls) were at risk, but neither drugs nor prostitution killed them. You did. You killed them, stripped them and left them... Why you did it may never be known.' The judge added: 'It is right you should spend your whole life in prison. This was a targeted campaign of murder (which entailed) a substantial degree of pre-meditation and planning.'

In view of the judge's wish that he should die behind bars, a suicide watch was put on Wright from the moment he entered Britain's highest security prison, Belmarsh, in southeast London. Meanwhile, police kept open the possibility that the 49-year-old killer may have been involved in other cases, including one of Britain's most notorious unsolved mysteries: the disappearance of estate agent Suzy Lamplugh in 1986. It emerged that Wright knew Miss Lamplugh after they worked together on the *QE2*.

RIGHT: Detective Superintendent Stewart Gull makes a statement to the media following Wright's conviction on February 21, 2008.

Aileen Wuornos

In the end, Aileen Wuornos chose death over Death Row. She effectively volunteered for her own execution. After dropping all appeals and dismissing the lawyers who were pleading her insanity, she petitioned the state for an early execution. She was described as being 'in a good mood' during her last hours. And at 9.47am on October 9, 2002, she got her wish when, at the age of 46, she was pronounced dead by lethal injection in Florida State Prison, near Starke.

Why I Hate Human Life, By The 'Damsel Of Death'

Confessing to seven murders, Wuornos was America's 'first female serial killer'—in the sense that she was the first female ever to fit the FBI profile of that normally exclusively male breed. Given her early upbringing, it would have been a miracle if her life had been anything but disturbed. Aileen was born in a Detroit suburb in 1956 to a mother who had married two years before at the age of 14 and a father she never met because he was in jail for raping a seven-year-old girl. When she was four, she was abandoned by her

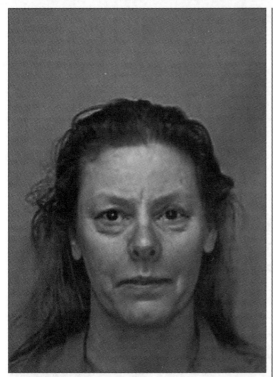

ABOVE: Aileen Wuornos was described by her own defense counsel as being 'the most disturbed individual I have ever represented'.

up in Florida where she had a longstanding lesbian relationship with a woman named Tyria Moore, surviving on the proceeds of Wuornos's prostitution.

Wuornos did not embark on her brief killing spree until November 1989, when she packed a pistol in her purse and flagged down a store owner near Daytona Beach. She robbed him and shot him dead. In May 1990, she shot a construction worker who stopped his pickup truck at a roadside near Gainesville. In June, another body turned up, this time near Tampa—naked and with nine bullet holes in it. The same month, a 65-year-old missionary was murdered near Jupiter. In August, a delivery driver was shot twice in the Ocala Forest. In September, a retired police chief was shot seven times and dumped in a vacant lot in Ocala. That same month, a truck driver was found shot through the head near Cross City.

The victims of Wuornos's two-year murder rampage were all middle-aged white men who had made the mistake of picking up the gun-toting hooker on the road. In each murder, Wuornos had followed the same pattern of flagging down men who were driving alone on or near Interstate 75.

Police finally caught up with Wuornos in a biker bar in January 1991. She confessed to the seven murders, claiming the men had tried to rape her and that she had killed them in self-defense. Now tagged the 'Damsel of Death', she was tried at Daytona Beach in January 1992 for only her first murder, of the store owner. Wuornos, who was distraught when her ex-lover Tyria Moore appeared as a witness for the prosecution, nevertheless showed no remorse as she was found guilty, with a jury recommendation for the death penalty. Her counsel afterward described her as 'the most disturbed individual I have represented'.

As other indictments were added, Wuornos told the Florida Supreme Court: 'I'm one who seriously hates human life and would kill again.' However, during her 10 years on Death Row, she became a born-again Christian and said she would welcome paying the ultimate penalty. Despite concerns about the execution of potentially mentally ill prisoners, Florida Governor Jeb Bush finally lifted his stay of execution after three state-appointed psychiatrists concluded that Wuornos was 'lucid and cognisant' and ready to die.

mother and was raised by her grandparents.

She endured a childhood of physical abuse at the hands of her grandfather and of sexual abuse by neighborhood boys. At 14, she was raped and became pregnant. At 15, her grandmother died and her grandfather threw her out of the house, calling her 'a whore'. She gave her son up for adoption at birth and began a life of petty crime and prostitution.

In 1976, Wuornos was picked up while hitch-hiking by a millionaire 50 years her senior and they married soon afterward. When her husband refused to give her money to fund her wild nights on the town, she beat him up. He successfully filed for divorce. Thus, at the age of 20, Aileen Wuornos was back on the road: a drunk, a drifter, a petty thief, and fraudster. She ended

ABOVE: The hearse carrying Wuornos's body leaves the Florida State Prison following her execution by lethal injection on October 9, 2002.

Graham Young

Even as a schoolboy, Graham Young demonstrated a sinister bent. He developed a passion for poisons, reading up on infamous villains like the wife killer Dr William Palmer (see page 155). Young's father Fred inadvertently encouraged him by buying him a chemistry set.

Danger Signs Ignored Over 'Teacup Poisoner'

Even at the age of 13, Young's comprehensive knowledge of toxicology enabled him to convince a local pharmacist in St Albans, Hertfordshire, that he was 17, and he procured a dangerous quantity of the poisons antimony, digitalis, and arsenic and the heavy metal, thallium, for 'study' purposes. He began carrying a phial of the poison around with him at all times, referring to it as 'my little friend'.

Eager to put his knowledge to the test, his first victim, a school pal, became seriously ill after his sandwiches were laced with antimony but survived. In 1961, his elder sister was found to have been poisoned by belladonna but also survived. The following year, his stepmother was found by her husband writhing in agony in the back garden of their home, with Young looking on in fascination. She died in hospital and her body was cremated. Fred Young was next to suffer attacks of vomiting and excruciating cramps, and he was admitted to hospital where he was diagnosed with antimony poisoning.

It was Young's chemistry teacher who, suspecting his pupil's murderous intent, tipped off the police. Sessions with a police psychiatrist confirmed that he was a serial killer in the making but no murder charges could be brought against him because his stepmother's cremation had destroyed the evidence. Still only 15, he was committed to Broadmoor maximum-security hospital, the youngest inmate since 1885, for a minimum period of 15 years.

ABOVE: John Tilson, one of the surviving victims of serial poisoner Graham Young, outside St Albans Crown Court in June 1972.

Within weeks, a fellow inmate died of poisoning by cyanide, which Young claimed to have extracted from laurel bush leaves. The killer was not taken seriously and the death was recorded as 'suicide'. Another record on his file shows that in 1970, when recommended for early release, he told a psychiatric nurse that he planned to kill one person for every year he had been in Broadmoor.

Amazingly, he was still freed after nine years' incarceration and obtained a job with a company manufacturing photographic instruments. Within weeks, staff began to be struck down with a mystery disease. Of the 70 people affected, three died in four months. During a company investigation, Young could not resist revealing his knowledge of chemicals and Scotland Yard were contacted.

ABOVE: Graham Young's fascination with causing pain and death through the administering of poison began in childhood.

Young was accused of two murders, two attempted murders and two cases of administering poison. The case was clear-cut, and a single entry in his diary, relating to the death of one of his work colleagues, would have sealed his fate: 'I have administered a fatal dose of the special compound to F. and anticipate a report on his progress on Monday. I gave him three separate doses.'

He pleaded not guilty, relishing his moment of notoriety in the dock—although he was unhappy that the press had labeled him the 'Teacup Poisoner', believing that 'World Poisoner' would better fit his infamy. On June 29, 1972, the jury at St Albans Crown Court took less than an hour to find him guilty, and he was given four life sentences. In August 1990, warders at Parkhurst Prison found 42-year-old Young dead of a heart attack on the floor of his cell.

Zodiac Killer

Random and motiveless, they are the most difficult serial murder cases to solve. San Francisco endured a brief reign of terror in 1968 and 1969, during which time a ruthless killer slew five people and wounded two more. The killings were followed by detailed descriptions of the atrocities in letters to newspapers, signed by a cross placed on a circle: the symbol of the Zodiac.

Motiveless Crimes Grip San Francisco

The first murders firmly attributed to the 'Zodiac Killer' were of a student couple, aged 16 and 17, who were shot in a quiet lane near Vallejo, near San Francisco, in December 1968. The pair had apparently

BELOW: One of the Zodiac Killer's coded messages which contained the hidden script: 'I like killing people'.

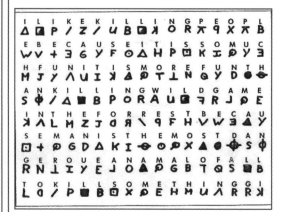

LEFT: One of the letters sent to a San Francisco newspaper by the Zodiac Killer, featuring his trademark signature.

ABOVE: Three of the Zodiac's victims. Left to right: cab driver Paul Stine, Cecilia Shepard, and Bryan Hartnell, who survived.
BELOW: Two homicide detectives inspect the clothes of a murder victim at a San Francisco morgue in March 1974.

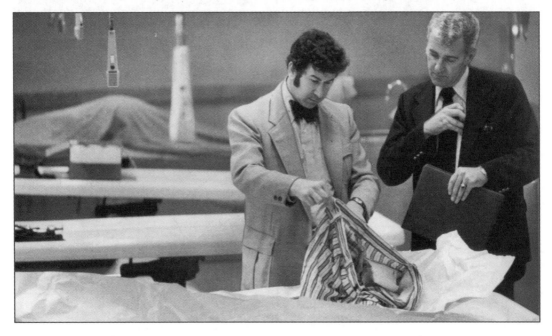

ABOVE: A card sent by the Zodiac Killer to Paul Avery, a reporter on the *San Francisco Chronicle*.

said, 'I like killing people' and added that 'when I die I will be reborn in paradise and those I have killed will become my slaves'.

'Zodiac' fell silent again until September 1969 when the gruff voice at the end of the phone line directed police to the shore of Lake Berryessa, in the Napa Valley, where two students, a girl of 22 and her boyfriend aged 20, had been killed in a frenzied attack. The assailant had daubed the zodiac sign on the side of the couple's white car, along with the dates of the previous murders. The girl, who had been stabbed with a foot-long bayonet 24 times, died in hospital two days later; her boyfriend, with bayonet wounds in the back, survived. He described the attacker as wearing a black hood with slits for his mouth and eyes.

'Zodiac' moved onto the streets of San Francisco itself

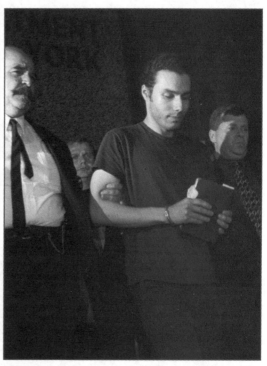

ABOVE: Police arrest Heriberto Seda, a copycat killer from 1990. Seda planned to kill one person from each of the 12 astrological signs.

been fleeing from their car when gunned down, but there was no obvious motive for the crime.

A similar double shooting followed the next July. The gunman had driven up alongside a car and opened fire without warning, killing a 22-year-old girl and seriously injuring her 19-year-old boyfriend. Police were alerted to the crime by a call from a man, described as having a 'gruff voice', who boasted: 'I also killed those kids last year.'

Following this attack, three newspapers received coded notes which, when matched and decoded, provided a weird message from 'Zodiac' in which he to strike again two weeks later, shooting a 29-year-old student and part-time taxi driver as he sat in a cab. The gunman, described by witnesses as short, in his 40s, with thick horn-rimmed glasses and crew-cut brown hair, fled into side-streets pursued by two patrolmen and escaped in the wooded military reservation known as The Presidio. The shooting was followed by letters to newspapers, this time enclosing a shred of bloodstained shirt torn from the victim—and claiming, not the five slayings attributed to him, but eight murders so far.

The 'Zodiac Killer' next struck in March 1970 when a 23-year-old woman was traveling toward Petaluma, northwest of San Francisco, when another driver flagged her down, told her that one of her rear wheels was wobbling and offered her a ride. Once in his car, he warned her: 'You know you're going to die—you know I'm going to kill you.' As he slowed, she leapt out and flagged down another car. Her description exactly fitted the taxi driver's killer.

Again, 'Zodiac' wrote to newspapers, acknowledging the kidnap attempt and upping his claimed victims to 37. The last letter was sent in April 1974. Since then, nothing…and the identity of the 'Zodiac Killer' has remained one of the greatest unsolved mysteries of modern crime.

Hans Van Zom

Hans Van Zon was a wastrel, a fantasist, a liar, and a cheat. But he had one asset that compensated for these deficiencies: he was absolutely charming. It won him admirers and lovers among both men and women, some of whom paid for this trust with their lives.

Fantasist Who Couldn't Take Failure

Johannes Marinus (Hans) van Zon was born of working-class parents in Utrecht, Holland, in April 1942. He was intelligent but there was no cash to advance his education and, at the age of 16, he turned to crime, first as a minor confidence trickster, then as a burglar.

Van Zon realized that he had homosexual tendencies but tried to hide them. In 1964 he dated Elly Hager-Segor but, after his first failed attempt at lovemaking, she called off the affair. Spurned, he strangled her before slitting her throat with a bread knife. His next love affair was with a homosexual movie director, Claude Berkeley, whom he met in Amsterdam in 1965. That relationship also failed and the man was similarly dispatched by his lover.

Shortly after the slaying, Van Zon married a chambermaid, Italian-born Caroline Gigli, 47, who supported both of them on her meager wages. After an attempt to kill her, his wife went to the police, who put him in jail for a month. But it was not his wife who was to be his next victim; Van Zon was keeping a 37-year-old mistress, Coby van der Voort—and was making money on the side by selling pornographic photographs of both his wife and girlfriend.

When Coby tried to end their affair in April 1967, Van Zon fed her barbiturates, pretending they were aphrodisiac pills, before smashing her skull with a lead pipe and finishing her off by slashing her throat with the familiar bread knife. He tried to fool police by making the murder look like a bungled burglary, stealing items of Coby's jewelry and handing them to Caroline.

Van Zon was now living in a total fantasy world. He claimed to be, variously, a fashion designer, private detective, movie star business tycoon, and a CIA spy. He could not help boasting about his killings to an ex-convict, Arnoldus Rietbergen, nicknamed 'Old Nol', who used the information to 'persuade' Van Zon to commit other murders for profit. Those known about are the death of a girl in May 1967 and of a farmer that same August.

Van Zon and Rietbergen were caught in December when blows from the lead piping failed to kill their final victim, an elderly lady. In March 1970, a Utrecht court sentenced Van Zon to life, with a minimum of 20 years, and his accomplice to seven years.

Anna Zwanziger

Poor Anna Schoenleben, born in Nuremberg, Germany, in 1760, did not have much going for her. A contemporary report described her as 'ugly, stunted, without attraction of face, figure, speech; a misshapen woman whom some people likened to a toad'. It would seem that she was lucky to have ever found a husband, but the marriage ended in misery. Herr Zwanziger, a successful lawyer, was a violent bully who spent her inheritance on drink.

Poisonous 'Toad' Dies By The Sword

Anna was forced into prostitution to support herself and two children, although she insisted to her friends that she only ever slept with 'gentlemen'. Upon the death of her husband through alcoholism, she advertised herself as a housekeeper and cook to the Bavarian judiciary and, from their elevated ranks, set about finding a new husband.

There was one flaw in her plan: each of the judges she went to work for was already married or engaged. Anna's solution was simple; she set about ridding herself of all rivals to her affections by poisoning two of the women, along with one of the judges, his guests, several servants, and a baby.

The widow's first potential husband was a judge named Glaser who, although separated, was still married. Anna engineered a reconciliation between the couple and, once the wife had returned to the marital home, fed her arsenic in her tea until she died. In the process, Anna also poisoned several of the judge's guests, although they survived.

Her next victim was another judge, named Grohmann, whom Anna killed when she discovered that he had wedding plans which did not involve her. He died an agonizing death after being served a bowl of soup. Anna also put arsenic in the drink of three servants who had upset her, although they survived.

Her third employer, Judge Gebhard, refused to believe his sickly wife's claims that food tasted strange since the arrival of their new housekeeper. It was only when he himself found a white sediment in his brandy glass that he became suspicious. It was too late. His wife died in convulsions. So did their baby after Anna fed the infant a biscuit dipped in arsenic-laced milk. Again, the servants were also poisoned but survived. Judge Gebhard had their food analyzed and traces of arsenic were found. By now, Anna had fled—but not before lacing every salt and sugar shaker in the house with arsenic.

Anna Zwanziger was arrested in October 1809 after police exhumed her victims' bodies and discovered traces of the poison. The poisoner had foolishly led them to her by writing letters to the Gebhard family asking if she could have her old job back. She eventually confessed, admitting: 'Yes, I killed them all and would have killed more if I had the chance.' She referred to arsenic as 'my truest friend' and said she 'trembled with pleasure' when handling it.

Before being beheaded by the sword in July 1811, she told her prison warders: 'It is perhaps better for the community that I should die, as it would be impossible for me to give up the practice of poisoning people.'

Marquise De Brinvilliers

Marie-Madeleine-Marguerite, Marquise de Brinvilliers was the eldest of five children in the French aristocratic 17th century family d'Aubray. The daughter of Viscount Antoine Dreux d'Aubray, a civil lieutenant of Paris, she was married in 1651 at the age of 21, to a married army officer, Antoine Gobelin de Brinvilliers, a gambling womanizer who paid her little attention. As a result, she took a lover, one Chevalier Jean-Baptiste de Sainte-Croix, an army captain and friend of her father.

Libertine Who Learned The Art Of Poison

Outraged by his daughter's affair with a trusted family friend, the old man forbade her from seeing Sainte-Croix, and in 1663 had him thrown into the Bastille. On his release, however, the lovers were reunited and plotted to take revenge on d'Aubray—and at the same time ensure her inheritance. In the Bastille, Sainte-Croix had learned the art of poisoning. With the assistance of one of the royal apothecaries to the court of King Louis XIV, he obtained tasteless but lethal potions, which Marie fed to her father, who in 1666 became her victim.

With her high-spending habits, Marie's share of Viscount d'Aubray's inheritance did not last long, and when the money ran out, she turned her attention to the rest of the family. Her elder brother died in 1670, followed by her younger brother and then her sister and sister-in-law. Former lovers suffered the same fate. Marie's husband survived but was prone to mysterious illnesses. Ruthlessly, Marie perfected her poison techniques on as many as 50 people during 'mercy missions' visiting the sick in a local hospital. The marquise was finally exposed when her lover Sainte-Croix died in 1672. He left instructions that a box should be delivered to his mistress, Marie, but his wife opened it and saw a variety of poisons and incriminating papers.

Marie went on the run but was arrested in Liege. Under interrogation, she threatened: 'Half the people of quality are involved in this sort of thing, and I could

ABOVE: An artist's impression of jailers torturing the Marquise de Brinvilliers with the 'water cure'.

ruin them if I were to talk.' The once haughty libertine was brutally tortured, her jailers mainly employing what was known as 'the water cure'—in which she was forced to drink 16 pints (9 liters) of water. Tried in Paris in 1676 and found guilty, she was executed, her body and severed head being thrown onto a fire.

Many members of the French nobility breathed a sigh of relief at her death because, while confessing her own guilt, she had refused to name other aristocrats caught up in sex scandals. The dramatic and romantic mysteries surrounding the case have since inspired poet Robert Browning (*The Poisoner*) and several authors, including Alexandre Dumas (*The Marquise de Brinvilliers*) and Arthur Conan Doyle (*The Leather Funnel*).

Richard Ramírez

The spooky killer known as the 'Night Stalker' was an avowed Satanist who terrorized the streets of Los Angeles for 13 months from 1984–85. Richard Ramírez would creep into a house at night, shoot or strangle any adult males and then subject women and children to sadistic rape and mutilation. Occasionally he would leave his mark as the 'Devil's Disciple'—an inverted pentagram scrawled on a mirror or wall. He also used to draw occult signs on the victims' bodies.

Fan Mail Galore For The 'Night Stalker'

ABOVE: A police mugshot of Richard Ramírez. The Mexican was fascinated by death from an early age.

Ricardo Múñoz Ramírez was born in El Paso, Texas, the son of Mexican immigrants. At an early age, he was fascinated by death and would spend nights in cemeteries. At 12, he fell under the influence of a cousin, a Vietnam War veteran who told tales of killing and torturing civilian women. According to later testimony, the cousin murdered his own wife while Ramírez was in the same room.

ABOVE: Ramírez, appearing to revel in his notoriety, wears sunglasses during a court appearance.

ABOVE: After his conviction the killer proclaimed: 'I will be avenged. Lucifer dwells within all of us.'

In his teens, Ramírez turned to crime and drugs. A police profile described him as 'a confused, angry loner who sought refuge in thievery, drugs, the dark side of rock music, and finally murder and rape'.

Upon moving to Los Angeles, Ramírez committed his first 'Night Stalker' murder in June 1984 when, high on cocaine, he crept into the apartment of a 79-year-old woman, stabbed her repeatedly, almost decapitating her, then sexually assaulted her. He was responsible for at least 18 further killings, his victims' ages ranging from the early 30s to the 70s. The methods he used were varied but included shooting, bludgeoning, throat cutting, and battering to death. Although the attacks

RIGHT: Ramírez in court with one of his calling cards, an inverted pentagram, drawn on his left palm.

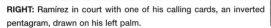

satisfied Ramírez's sadistic sexual urges, he also stole from those he killed.

Police finally got lucky in August 1985 when they found a fingerprint in a getaway car used for one of the attacks and matched it to Ramírez, then aged 25 and a known petty criminal. His photograph was circulated to the press—and had an instant result. Ramírez was recognized as he tried to drag a woman out of her car in a Los Angeles suburb. He was attacked by the woman's husband and by a gathering mob, who turned him over to the cops bruised and bleeding.

After one of the lengthiest murder trials in American history, Ramírez was found guilty in September 1989 of 13 murders, five attempted murders, 11 sexual assaults, and 14 burglaries. He was sentenced to death in California's gas chamber and, as he left the courtroom for San Quentin's Death Row, he snarled: 'You maggots make me sick. I will be avenged. Lucifer dwells within all of us.' Of the death sentence he joked: 'Big deal. Death comes with the territory. See you in Disneyland.'

Inexplicably, the 'Night Stalker' trial had generated an amazing amount of fan mail for Ramírez. One besotted woman, Doreen Lioy, who wrote him 75 letters, won a proposal of marriage. With California's death sentences seemingly permanently stalled, the couple were wed in San Quentin in 1996.

David Parker Ray

David Parker Ray is the serial killer who was never convicted of a single slaying, although his tally of female victims may be as high as 60; they died in the most horrific circumstances after kidnap, captivity, abuse, rape, and torture. Yet he escaped the full weight of justice, dying in 2002 of heart failure after just three years in prison on charges that all fell short of murder.

How Many Innocents Lured To 'Satan's Den'?

Ray was a loner with four failed marriages who built a torture chamber in a trailer at the back of his home. There, in what he referred to as his 'Satan's Den' or 'The Toy Box', his victims were drugged and chained to a gynecological chair fitted with straps and surrounded by an array of torture instruments and sex toys.

Ray's reign of terror ended in March 1999 when one of his victims, Cynthia Vigil, escaped from him and ran through the streets of Elephant Butte, New Mexico, naked, with a metal collar around her neck and trailing a chain. The sobbing 21-year-old had been held captive for three days and subjected to a terrifying ordeal of rape and torture.

Police arrested Ray, a 59-year-old park warden and mechanic, and searched his home and backyard den. A policeman said: 'There were sadistic pictures on the walls, straps and chains, a bar he'd labeled "ankle stretcher", sex toys attached to power drills, dildos with nails embedded in them. Everything in that trailer denoted pain.'

Officers found a tape recording in which Ray explained to his victims what he was about to do to them, saying that he had 'no qualms about slitting your throat' because 'you're a piece of meat to me'. On the tape, he talked of 37 previous abductions.

Police also examined videotapes containing footage of one of Ray's victims strapped to the chair. Apparently drugged, she could be identified only by an unusual tattoo on her leg. When the tattoo was shown on TV, a 25-year-old woman, Kelly Van Cleave, identified herself—but said she was confused because she had no memory of being held captive. It was only under police questioning that her memory partially returned and, horrified, she realized that the nightmares she had been suffering were of real events and that she had been drugged to prevent her from recalling the horrors of her captivity.

Police suspected that Ray may have slain as many as 60 women but, when a search of the area revealed not a single body, prosecutors decided a murder charge was impossible. Instead, Ray was charged with kidnapping, rape, and torture.

He almost escaped justice entirely, because the two principal witnesses were deemed potentially unreliable, Kelly Van Cleave still having only partial memories of her experience and Cynthia Vigil being a heroin-addicted prostitute. Moreover, at Ray's trial in July 2000, the judge ruled that the incriminating tape recording was inadmissible. The trial ended in a hung jury.

A retrial nine months later produced a different verdict. On April 16, 2001, the jury were unanimous.

ABOVE: The smart appearance of Ray during his trial belied a man capable of remorseless evil.

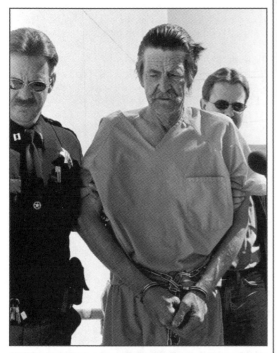

ABOVE: David Parker Ray, shackled by police officers after his arrest. He was later sentenced to 224 years in jail.

David Parker Ray was jailed for 224 years, less the two and a half years he had already spent in prison. On May 28, 2002, just eight months into his sentence, David Parker Ray died of heart failure.

Earlier, in other trials, three of Ray's accomplices received lesser sentences after plea deals involving giving evidence against him. Dennis Roy Yancy confessed to strangling to death another kidnap victim, 22-year-old Marie Parker, whose body was never found, and was jailed for 20 years. Ray's live-in girlfriend Cynthia Hendy confessed to being an accessory and received 36 years. Ray's daughter Jessy was convicted of helping her father kidnap and torture Kelly Van Cleave but was released with five years' probation under a deal that her father forewent his right to appeal.

Picture Credits

Getty Images
12 (both), 13, 14 Hulton Archive
15 Doug Pensinger
18 (left) Hulton Archive, (right) Keystone/
Hulton Archive
19 (top) BIPS/Hulton Archive, (bottom) Mitchell
20 (top) Keystone/Hulton Archive,
(bottom) Nixon/Express
22 Robert Harding World Imagery
30 Maxim Marmur/AFP
31 Kostya Smirnov/AFP
33 (left) Keystone/Hulton Archive, (right) Express
34 Keystone
35 (left) Keystone/Hulton Archive,
(right) Jack Hickes/Keystone/Hulton Archive
36 (top) Keystone, (bottom) Jack Hickes/Keystone/
Hulton Archive
37 Keystone
40 (both) Keystone/Hulton Archive
41 (left) Express, (right) Keystone
42 J. A. Hampton/Topical Press Agency
43 (left) Topical Press Agency/Hulton Archive,
(right) Topical Press Agency
44 (top left, right) Hulton Archive,
(bottom left) Topical Press Agency
45 Hulton Archive
49 (both) Evening Standard
50 (top left) Hulton Archive, (bottom right) California
Department of Corrections and Rehabilitation,
51 (top) Michael Ochs Archives
52 (top left) Express Newspapers,
(bottom right) Hulton Archive
54 (both), 55 Patrick Riviere
58 (bottom right), 59 (top right) Keystone/
Hulton Archive
63 Hulton Archive
64 (top) Illustrated London News/Hulton Archive,
(bottom) Hulton Archive
68, 69 (top) Keystone, (bottom right) AFP
70 Keystone
83 Florida DOC

84 Chris Livingston
85 (both) Keystone/Hulton Archive

iStock
32 iStockphoto.com/cglow

Press Association
38, 47 (both), 61, 62, 71, 72, 79, 80 (all) Suffolk Police,
81 (left), (top right) Elizabeth Cook, (bottom right)
ANPR, 82, 87 (both), 88 (both).

Every effort has been made to trace the ownership of
copyrighted material and to secure permission from
copyright holders. In the event of any question arising
as to the use of any material, we will be pleased to make
necessary corrections in future printings.

To Katie, Leonie and Mike
Who, in the interests of research, braved more gore and
guts than any homicide detective would experience in
a lifetime. My sincere thanks to them.